M000102105

Brassey's *History of Uniforms*

Current titles

American Civil War: Confederate Army
American Civil War: Union Army

Forthcoming titles

Napoleonic Wars: Wellington's Army
Napoleonic Wars: Napoleon's Army
Mexican-American War 1846-48
English Civil War

Brassey's *History of Uniforms*

American Civil War Union Army

By Robin Smith

Colour plates by Chris Collingwood

Series editor Tim Newark

To Jean Smith

First English Edition 1996

UK editorial offices: Brassey's Ltd, 33 John Street, London
WC1N 2AT
UK Orders: Marston Book Services, PO Box 269, Abingdon,
Oxford OX14 4SD

North American Orders: Brassey's Inc,
PO Box 960, Herndon, VA 22070, USA

Robin Smith has asserted his moral right to be identified as
the author of this work.

Library of Congress Cataloging in Publication Data available
British Library Cataloguing in Publication Data
A catalogue record for this book is available from the British
Library

ISBN 1 85753 174 4 Hardcover

Typeset and printed in Great Britain by Images Book
Production Ltd.

Contents

Introduction

In 1861 the regular United States Army only number-13,000 strong in all arms, barely the strength of a single division. Since the end of the American Revolution, the United States had never maintained a large standing army during peacetime. Before the outbreak of the Civil War, over 180 of its 198 infantry, artillery and cavalry units were stationed in more than 100 small frontier posts, and the strength of the army was further eroded when more than 300 officers resigned to join the Confederacy. It had to draw on the large reservoir of volunteers that existed either in the many pre-war militia units that almost every town or city had, or in the units that were raised virtually overnight to meet President Lincoln's call in April 1861, for 75,000 volunteers to fight the South.

Heavily influenced by the North's greater interest in Zouave and Chasseur uniforms, many of these units wore a variety of dress. This variety, together with the creation of specialist units, like Colonel Hiram Berdan's green-clad sharpshooters, meant Union uniforms matched the range of dress found in the Confederacy. The Union Army eventually comprised some 2,772,408 men and was the largest force raised in the country until the United States mobilised its forces for World War One. In many ways, American Civil War uniforms represent a transition period between the gaudy uniforms of the Napoleonic era and the functional dress of the First World War.

The official responsibility for providing uniforms for the United States Army lay with the U.S. Army's Quartermaster Department which had been supervising the design and manufacturing of clothing for regular troops at the Schuylkill Arsenal in Pennsylvania since the War of 1812. But the regular army was so small that its influence on uniforms in a country which blossomed with volunteer militia units was often limited. Many of the individual companies in the militia designed their own uniforms, but some large cities like New York uniformed all the companies of a volunteer battalion or regiment alike and many states based a large proportion of their dress regulations on those laid down by the United States War Department.

When President Lincoln issued his call for 75,000 volunteers to serve for three months, the War Department quickly realised that many volunteer regiments lacked even the most basic uniform and equipment items. The Quartermaster Department was authorised to provide volunteer troops with cheap basic clothing, but the supplies just weren't there. It was recommended that the States furnished their own clothing supplies and be reimbursed by the government. Some States responded efficiently, others less so. In the scramble to provide uniforms, corruption flourished with some unscrupulous contractors out to make easy money.

Some early war uniforms were made of a cheap material called shoddy which would literally fall apart at the seams and disintegrate. The popular magazine *Harper's Weekly* described it as: 'a villainous compound, the refuse stuff and sweepings of the shop, pounded, rolled, glued and smoothed to the external form and gloss of cloth, but no more like the genuine article than the shadow is to the substance. Soldiers on the first day's march or in the earliest storm, found their clothes, overcoats and blankets scattering to the wind in rags or dissolving into their primitive elements of dust under the pelting rain.'

The New York authorities decided to give their troops a standardised outfit with a smart dark blue jacket and ordered more than 32,000 of these jackets from nine different contractors. But there was a shortage of dark blue cloth, so the New York tailors Brooks Brothers, was authorised to produce over 7,000 grey jackets instead. Soldiers claimed that not only did the jackets fall apart, but the coarse cloth irritated their skin. Meanwhile in Ohio, an enterprising tailor ran a uniform production line cutting out uniform parts from pieces of cloth which were then handed to a team of local ladies to be sewn together.

Many of the proud volunteers who received the uniforms, said they were about two feet too large across the chest but at least they were luckier than some volunteer outfits marching to defend Washington, who had no uniforms at all and precious little in the way of armaments. One regiment had to leave 200 of its men at home for want of weapons and some regular officers were very scathing about the quality of the volunteer troops. 'You might as well attempt to put out the flames of a burning house with a squirt gun,' sneered William Tecumseh Sherman.

The situation in supplying uniforms and equipment was to improve dramatically, once the hysteria of the first few months of the war calmed down. Cloth imports from abroad stimulated American manufacturers to improve standards, so much so that the Boston Board of Trade complained bitterly about the imports of foreign cloth, claiming that Northern industry was now sufficiently geared up to clothe the Union Army. They were right; by the end of 1861 Northern factories produced 550,000 uniforms.

The majority of uniforms worn by Northern soldiers were manufactured from wool. In the first half of the 19th Century the U.S. Army had issued linen or cotton fatigue uniforms to its men, but around 1853 the army stopped buying the material and only occasional issues were made after 1855. Officers' uniforms were usually of better quality broadcloth or serge, while kersey, a coarse cloth woven from wool was chiefly used in the manufacture of enlisted men's trousers. Linsey, a coarse wool material of inferior quality, was a feature of many uniforms manufactured in 1861 but was really only a couple of steps away from the notorious shoddy cloth.

The U.S. Army's uniform regulations of 1821 stated that dark blue should be the national colour of uniforms for American soldiers. Yet during the Mexican War of 1846 to 1848 the fatigue uniforms of most of the soldiers were mainly sky blue material which was much easier to get hold of and cheaper to manufacture. From 1858-1861 the army wore dark blue coats and dark blue trousers, but in the early stages of the Civil War it was suggested that issuing cheaper sky blue trousers could save the hard pressed Union treasury $750,000 a year. Some American military thinkers of the time also wanted to outfit the regular army in sky blue jackets, but the only regular Northern unit ever to wear sky blue jackets was the Invalid Corps formed in 1863 from wounded veterans who performed light duties.

A curious aspect of some Civil War uniforms worn

This photograph of a private of the 10th U.S. Infantry taken in the 1850s, shows all the finery of pre-Civil War American soldiers and the French influences in uniforms that continued all the way through the Civil War. The 10th U.S. Infantry was organised in 1855 and the Private wears a regulation frock coat cut in the French *Chasseur à pied* pattern. The coat has light blue piping and brass shoulder scales. On show beside the private is his full dress hat or shako. These hats were made of felt stretched over a cardboard or paper base, but some were made entirely out of leather. Just visible on the hat is a light blue welt and pompom, which like the trim on the private's coat designates that he is an infantryman. David Scheinmann.

by Union volunteers is that while the majority were outfitted in blue uniforms some units wore grey, leading to potential disasters on the battlefield against a largely grey clad enemy. Grey had been a popular colour with many Northern militia units before the war, including volunteers from Maine, Vermont and Wisconsin who proudly held on to their uniforms at the beginning of the conflict. But by the middle of 1862, no grey clad Northern troops could be found on the battlefield. Good sense had at last prevailed.

Zouaves and Militia Units

By the mid 19th Century, the French Army had a tremendous influence on military dress worldwide, especially in America. The traditional bond with the United States forged during the American Revolution, when France supported the fledging country in its

This distinctive looking officer circa 1855, wears epaulettes and what appears to be a non-regulation large bow tie. His trousers seem to follow the rather straight cut of the 1850s and his shako on the table beside him has a feather plume and eagle insignia. The unidentified officer is probably an officer with a militia unit and the sword he carries is an 1820s pattern. Possibly it may even have been handed down to him. David Scheinmann.

fight for independence, and later the glowing reputation of French troops in the Crimea, was particularly noticeable in the many exotic French style uniforms worn by Northern volunteers. The most famous of these volunteer units were the many Northern Zouave regiments and companies, based on the famed Zouaves of the French Army whose reckless exploits during the Crimean War had won them much fame.

The original Zouaves were natives of the Zouaoua tribe of North Africa, particularly noted for their bravery who together with some French settlers were formed into two battalions and served with the French Army during France's North African campaigns in the 1830s. By the time of the Crimean War the ranks of the Zouaves were filled entirely by Frenchmen. Three Zouave regiments of the line had been created and a regiment of Imperial Guard Zouaves was raised in 1855. Union General George B. McClellan, who as a captain had been an American observer in the Crimea, called Zouaves the 'beau ideal of a soldier'.

On the eve of the American Civil War, a Zouave craze swept America started by Elmer E. Ellsworth, a penniless law student and military enthusiast who was so enthralled by the stories of Zouave exploits told to him by Charles A. DeVilliers, a former French Army surgeon who had served with a Zouave regiment in the Crimea, that he decided to form his own Zouave unit from a company of the Illinois State Militia. Several Zouave companies such as the company found

Opposite.
Unidentified Zouave, thought to be a member of the Phoenix Zouaves, a short lived Irish- American Zouave unit founded by Thomas Francis Meagher, who went on to form the Irish Zouaves of Company K, the 69th New York State Militia. For many years, illustrations of the uniform worn by Company K of the 69th have been erroneously based on those worn by the Phoenix Zouaves; but Company K never wore such elaborately decorated vests under their jackets. Michael J. McAfee.

This photograph of a 5th New Yorker was taken early in the war. Note the private's rolled blanket kept on top of his knapsack, and the badge, possibly his company's letter, on the front of his fez. There also appears to be another badge or piece of insignia attached to the front of his jacket. This man is completely uniformed and equipped ready for campaign, an enviable state for many soldiers as the war progressed. Brian C. Pohanka.

Hand tinted photo of a private of the 5th New York Volunteer Infantry, Duryée's Zouaves, the epitome of an exotically clad union volunteer. He has wrapped a turban around his fez and the fact that the tassel on the private's fez is very short and he's not wearing *jambieres* (leather greaves) over his white gaiters, indicates that this is a photograph also taken early in the war. Martin L. Schoenfeld.

in the Gardes Lafeyette, a militia unit largely composed of French immigrants in New York, already existed in America; but Ellsworth and his men who grandly called themselves the United States Zouave Cadets enthralled the public during a drill display tour of East Coast cities in 1860.

Ellsworth later raised the 11th New York

Volunteer Infantry, a unit of tough New York firemen who proudly called themselves Fire Zouaves, but Ellsworth and his men were destined not to see much glory. In Alexandria, Virginia, Ellsworth was gunned down and killed when he tried to remove a Confederate flag from a tavern and his dispirited men broke and ran when they came under heavy artillery fire at First Bull Run.

The classic French Zouave uniform was an adaptation of native North African dress comprising a fez, outlandish baggy trousers, and a short jacket worn over a shirt vest. The jacket was ornamented with trefoil designs called tombeaux on each side of the chest. The uniforms of American Zouaves varied from almost exact copies of French Zouave uniforms to wide interpretations of the Zouave style.

Ellsworth's first unit, the United States Zouave Cadets, wore no less than three styles of uniforms, but they were loosely based on French Chasseur uniforms and bore little resemblance to true Zouave uniforms, a point noted at the time in a report about the United States Zouave Cadets in the French newspaper *Courier des Etats Unis*: 'These Zouaves are, however, three quarters contraband. Their uniform has nothing, or rather very little of the uniform of the French corps whose name they have adopted.'

A company of the 5th New York photographed at their camp near Fortress Monroe, Virginia, in the summer of 1861. When British War correspondent, William Howard Russell, saw the 5th on parade he claimed that many of them were not wearing fezzes, but just turbans that looked like discoloured napkins wrapped around their heads, giving them a less than soldierly appearance. Brian C. Pohanka.

The same can be said of the New York Fire Zouaves, the second unit raised by Ellsworth, who were originally outfitted in grey jackets of a Chasseur pattern, and blue trousers. The jackets quickly wore out but the men kept their blue trousers and were issued with fezzes and blue waist sashes. A distinctive feature of the Fire Zouaves' uniforms were the red firemen's shirts they proudly wore. The men also shaved their heads like the French Zouaves.

Nearly every Northern State or town boasted Zouaves, even out West in Indiana, where the most famous Zouave regiment was Wallace's Zouaves founded by Colonel Lew Wallace, who was later to find fame as the author of the novel *Ben Hur*. Wallace was greatly impressed with the Zouave ideal, but as a devout Christian he didn't want his men dressed in Moslem clothing as represented by the true Zouave uniform, so his men were orginally dressed in grey

Lieutenant Colonel Noah Lane Farnham, the second commander of the 11th New York Volunteer Infantry, wears the grey Fire Zouaves officers' uniform. A stripe which was gold edged red is just visible on the seam of his trousers and the shoulder straps on his grey double breasted field officer's frock coat are dark blue with red edging. Farnham's pose for this portrait shot is remarkably casual, especially with his coat left open revealing his shirt. In mourning for Elmer E. Ellsworth, the Fire Zouaves' first commander who was gunned down in an Alexandria Tavern, Farnham wears a black armband. Brian C. Pohanka.

Opposite.
Reconstruction of a 5th New York, Duryée's Zouaves, on campaign 1862. This uniform with the distinctive red tombeaux on the chest separate from the red trim, is the third uniform issued to the regiment in February 1862 and the one most closely associated with the unit. The baggy trousers of the first uniform issued to Duryée's Zouaves featured blue trim around the pockets. Trousers issued later, like the ones worn in this picture, were plain. Paul Smith.

Chasseur pattern uniforms.

The most authentically dressed Union Zouave regiment was the famed 5th New York, Duryée's Zouaves. War observer General Prim of the Spanish Army said they looked exactly like the French 2nd Regiment of Zouaves after he inspected them.

The regiment was commanded by Colonel Abram Duryée, a big name in New York militia affairs. It was said that the 5th decided to adopt a full Zouave uniform when Felix Agnus a veteran of the French 2nd Regiment of Zouaves who had emigrated to America, wore his Zouave uniform when he enlisted with the Advance Guard, as Duryée's Zouaves were first known.

Regimental historian, Alfred Davenport, left this account of the 5th's uniform: 'A more picturesquely unique and fantastical costume could scarcely be conceived. The breeches were wide flowing Zouave pants of a bright red, narrow and pleated at the top, wide at the bottom and baggy in the rear. These were topped with a broad sash of the same colour edged with blue tape and falling nearly to the knee on the left side. The jacket was of a coarse blue material, trimmed with red tape, short, loose, low-necked and collarless and running in front. The shirts were of the same material with a broad stripe of red down the bosom. The leggings were heavy white canvas, buttoned to the knee and the shoes were clumsy, square toed scows. The caps were close-fitting red fezzes turned back from the top of the head, to which was attached a cord with a blue tassel that dangled down in the middle of the back.'

Some 5th New Yorkers complained that the first issue of uniforms was not of the best quality and poorly made, especially the baggy trousers which were cut too high in the calf, but the tailoring firm who made the uniforms said that some Zouaves were wearing ordinary trousers under the baggy pants which affected the drape. However, they did agree to lengthen the last 125 pairs they delivered by two inches.

The 5th New York's fezzes were manufactured by the Seamless Clothing Company and were of red felt

As befits his formal role, Gordon Winslow, the chaplain of the 5th New York wears the standard 5th New York officers' frockcoat with the waist sash that officers were ordered to wear in regimental orders made in May, 1861. His gauntlets though might have been a private purchase. Winslow's life ended tragically when he fell overboard from a steamer as he brought his wounded son, Cleveland, home. Cleveland had been a captain in the 5th New York before raising the 5th New York Veteran Volunteers. Brian C. Pohanka.

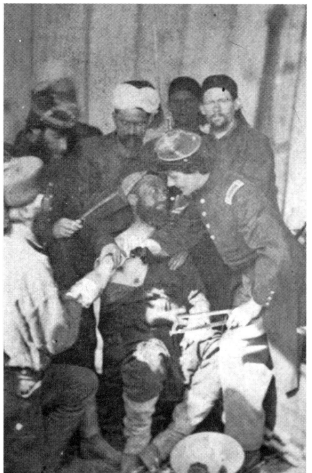

This grisly amputation scene is in fact a fake staged by 5th New York personnel. The officer wears a regulation dark blue frockcoat and note the elaborate gold braid decorations on his kepi. Photo spoofs like this, were not uncommon in the early war years. Brian C. Pohanka.

with a blue tassel. For ordinary wear the tassel was left to fall to the shoulder, but in action the cord could be drawn up through the fez to stop it getting in the way. For parade or as a matter of choice in the field, Zouaves wore white turbans around their fezzes. Despite its colourful uniforms, there were times when the 5th New York which served from 1861 to 1863, looked shabby. Indeed stories that Union soldiers were invariably better dressed than their Southern foes are a myth. As the experiences of the 5th *(continued on p. 23)*

Opposite.

Lorenzo Clark poses in the uniform worn by the Zouave company of the 74th New York Volunteer Infantry. Like Company K of the 69th New York, or Company B of the 13th Regiment New York State Militia, it was not unusual for a single company in a volunteer unit to wear Zouave dress. But not only did the 74th's Zouave company have ornate tombeuax designs on its jackets, they had tombeaux designs on either side of their vests, visible in this photo. Michael J. McAfee.

Above.
Distinctive 'flower' tombeaux were a feature of the Zouave uniforms worn by many Zouave regiments from Indiana and other parts of the West. Private A.G. Garrett of the 34th Indiana Veteran Volunteer Infantry, wears a jacket which has a 'false vest' sewn into it. His sleeves carry diagonal veteran's stripes, showing that Garrett signed up again after his original time of service expired. Michael J. McAfee.

Above Right.
James E. Taylor served with the 10th New York Volunteer Infantry, National Zouaves, until 1863. The 10th had quite a bewildering variety of uniforms during its existence, and in this photograph Taylor wears the distinctive dark blue kacket and light blue trousers of the 10th's last issued uniform. His trousers are tucked into white gaiters. Michael J. McAfee.

Opposite.
This sergeant of the 9th New York Volunteer Infantry, Hawkins' Zouaves, wears the uniform that became the standard issue Zouave uniform issued by the Army. The jackets were dark blue trimmed red and the matching dark blue trousers had ornamental red designs around the pockets. Either black or white gaiters were worn. Michael J. McAfee.

GROUP OF ELLSWORTH'S CHICAGO ZOUAVE CADETS.

No military organization during the war was more brilliant than the Chicago Zouave Cadets, with their striking and gay uniforms: their flowing red pants; their jaunty crimson caps; their peculiar drab gaiters and leggings, and the loose blue jackets, with rows of small, sparkling buttons, and the light-blue shirt beneath. In all their evolutions the Zouaves displayed great precision.

2nd Wisconsin Volunteer Infantry Regiment, Iron Brigade, Brawner's Farm, August 1862.

Comprising regiments from Wisconsin, Indiana and Michigan, the Iron Brigade was one of the most famous units of the American Civil War. During its time of service, the 2nd Wisconsin, who started the war in grey uniforms at First Bull Run, had the greatest number of deaths in battle of any regiment in the Union Army. One out of every five of its men never returned home.

The hatless private kneeling down is wearing an ordinary sack coat, the last resort of soldiers in many 'specialist' regiments whose uniforms were worn out or lost on campaign. The figures next to him wear the typical frock coats of the Iron Brigade and Hardee hats. These hats were ornamented with feather plumes, worn on either side, but under campaign conditions, many didn't last very long and were thrown away when they became tatty. However, based on evidence in contemporary photographs of Iron Brigade soldiers with plumes in their hats some months after their uniforms were issued, the soldiers illustrated in this plate have them. Many Iron Brigade soldiers like the two privates pictured here, wore brass eagle badges to secure the turned up sides of their hats. Most hats featured the infantry's distinctive bugle horn insignia worn on the front.

The 2nd Wisconsin lieutenant wears regulation officer's dress but instead of the Hardee also favoured by many officers of the Iron Brigade, he wears a forage cap. The lieutenant carries a .44 colt Army revolver and brandishes an imported German sword, the same pattern as an English rifle officer's sword of 1827 with a gothic hilt. Painting by Chris Collingwood.

Above.
Ellsworth's United States Zouave Cadets excited audiences with their theatrical drill displays on a grand tour in 1860. Here, they are pictured in their 'Zouave dress' which they wore for drill performances; one of four different styles of uniform the unit wore in its brief existence on the eve of the Civil War. The exact design on the Zouaves' shirts has puzzled many military historians. Contemporary photographs of the Zouave Cadets do not show it up well, but it appears to be a delicate floral pattern and the Zouaves' red trousers had a thin strip of gold running down the seams. The United States Zouave Cadets also wore a full dress uniform with white cross belts, a blue cap, blue frock coat and blue grey trousers. Both the frock coat and trousers were trimmed with buff piped red. A third style of uniform, the cadets' 'Chasseur dress', matched the frock coat with the red caps and red trousers of their Zouave dress. Peter Newark's Military Pictures.

Above.
Private Lee Matthews of the 76th Ohio Volunteer Infantry wears a particularly elaborate Zouave jacket, a style which was also worn by by the 53rd Ohio. This curious tombeaux design was one of the most elaborate of the Civil War. Michael J. McAfee.

Above Right.
This Corporal of the 140th New York Volunteer Infantry, also probably saw some particularly hard fighting in the Wilderness Campaign in the later stages of the War. The 140th's uniform was dark blue trimmed red and the soldier's false vest sewn

into the lining of his jacket, is clearly visible in this phototograph. The buckle on his waist belt is most likely a standard 'U.S.' or 'SNY' buckle. Michael J. McAfee.

Opposite.
The 155th Pennsylvania Volunteer Infantry wore a dark blue uniform with distinctive yellow tombeaux designs that show up well in this photograph of a private clutching his fez as he rests his hand on a studio prop. The arm wound this private received, might have been as a result of the terrible fight the 155th Pennsylvania took part in during the Wilderness Campaign. Michael J. McAfee.

22 Zouaves and Militia Units

Co. , 164 N.Y. vols.

A company of the 164th New York Volunteer Infantry look particularly fine on parade in uniforms patterned after those originally worn by Hawkins' Zouaves. Note the drummer boy also attired as a Zouave at the far left of the picture. Despite romantic stories of courage, drummer boys rarely accompanied their regiment into the thick of battle, but were usually ordered to fall out a safe distance from combat. Michael J. McAfee.

New York show, hard campaigning took its toll on both armies.

The 5th was mustered into the United States service on May 9 1861 and its uniforms were in a sorry state by the time the regiment arrived for a period of garrison duty in Baltimore Maryland in July 1861. Regimental historian Alfred Davenport wrote: 'Our men looked shabby, some of the uniforms being absolutely worthless.' In a letter to the Secretary of War dated July 27 1861 the regiment's commander Abram Duryée pleaded for something to be done about his men's clothing, writing: 'The uniforms furnished to us are nearly worn out and in a ruined condition.'

New uniforms for the regiment eventually arrived in September 1861, but they were not of good quality. Lieutenant Colonel Gouverneur Kemble Warren of the 5th bitterly complained that the linings of the

Opposite.
The 34th Ohio Volunteer Infantry, the Piatt Zouaves were renowned for wearing 18th century-style tricorne hats as part of their Zouave uniform but this ungainly looking duo prefer to wear fezzes. The jackets, which appear to be dark blue trimmed red, seem to be of a Chasseur style cut. Michael J. McAfee.

jackets were made out of a material that shrank and pulled the jackets out of shape if they became wet. New uniforms were issued in September 1861, but the following year the Zouaves were in a bad way again. Alfred Davenport left this description in a letter: 'Our regiment is ragged and ununiformed, wearing all kinds of clothes, they might either dress us up in our regular Zouave suit or give us the regulation uniform, the latter is much better for service, warmer and neater, but they seem disposed to give us neither, therefore we should have been naked long ago had we not bought pants from the regulars and other regiments who have plenty to spare.'

Despite these deprivations, the 5th New York and its successor regiments the 5th New York Veteran Battalion and the 165th New York, Second Battalion Duryée Zouaves, had admirable service records. Civil

Another view of the 164th, this time relaxing in camp with their arms stacked. It is claimed that the 164th had green tassels on their fezzes to show off their proud Irish heritage. Uniforms like these worn by the 164th, saw service with many National Guard Units in the years after the war had ended. Michael J. McAfee.

War Zouave regiments have sometimes been dismissed as nine day wonders, but they were active throughout the conflict. The uniform of the 9th New York Volunteer Infantry, Hawkins' Zouaves, with its dark blue trousers and dark blue jacket became the United States Quartermaster Department standard issue Zouave uniform worn by other regiments including the 164th New York. Surplus 9th New York Hawkins' Zouaves uniforms were also worn by some post war Militia units.

A regiment was even raised to honour Elmer Ellsworth, the man who had done so much to popularise Zouaves in America before his untimely death. Patriotic citizens of the Ellsworth Association nominated candidates for the 44th New York Volunteer Infantry, who were known as the People's Ellsworth Regiment or by the more spectacular title, Ellsworth's Avengers. Soldiers in the regiment had to be under 30 and stand not less than 5ft eight inches tall.

Their Zouave uniform comprising dark blue jackets and trousers and a red shirt trimmed blue was heavily influenced by the clothing worn by another unit the Albany Zouave Cadets. The men also received the standard regulation New York fatigue uniform of short dark blue jacket and sky blue trousers, but photos of enlisted men taken in Alexandria, Virginia in 1864 show them still wearing their popular Zouave dress.

Pennsylvania provided some fine Zouave regiments, notably the 114th Pennsylvania, the Collis Zouaves. In August 1861 Captain H. T. Collis raised a company of Zouaves called the Zouaves d'Afrique to act as bodyguard for General Nathaniel Banks and then he was commissioned to raise a full regiment of Zouaves, the 114th Pennsylvania. Collis Zouave musician Frank Rauscher described the uniform in his book *Music On The March*: 'The uniform adopted for the regiment was precisely like that of the original company - red pants, Zouave jacket, white leggings blue sash around the waist and white turbans, which pricked up the pride of the new recruits and gave the regiment an imposing and warlike appearance. The material for these uniforms was all imported from France, and special arrangements were made to secure a sufficient supply of the same to replenish the uniforms during the whole term of service.' It seems though that late in the war the men were forced to wear ordinary sky blue kersey trousers because supplies of scarlet cloth imported from France had run out.

During 1863 and 1864, the Union Army decided to transform three regiments who had been clad in ordinary army dress into Zouaves as a reward for their proficiency at drill and to maintain a Zouave esprit de corps. The regiments receiving these uniforms were the 146th New York in June 1863 and the 140th and 155th Pennsylvania who were issued with Zouave uniforms in the early part of 1864. 'The cloth is by far better material than any clothes issued before' wrote a private of the 140th New York. 'It is of good quality - the dark blue trimmed with red.'

The new uniforms were particularly welcome to the men of the 155th Pennsylvania who had begun

The men of 14th Regiment New York Sate Militia, the famous Red-legged Devils from Brooklyn, wore these distinctive kepis with red tops from the beginning of the war to the end. Many soldiers fixed brass numerals to the front, although judging from many contemporary photographs this practice doesn't seem to have been as widespread as previously thought. This kepi was worn during the war and the red dot in the centre of the top, is the badge of the 1st Corps in which the 14th Brooklyn served. Martin L. Schoenfeld.

These men of the 14th Brooklyn who had been baptised by fire at First Bull Run a few months before this photograph was taken, have the look of veterans and wear their uniforms accordingly. Note the narrowness of their Chasseur pattern trousers as compared with the fuller trousers worn by Zouave regiments and the fact that many of the men are not wearing the unit's characteristic gaiters. Author's collection.

Officers of the 14th Brooklyn wore regulation plain dark blue frock coats and red trousers with a gold stripe running down the outer seams of their trousers. Most of the officers in this photograph appear to be wearing kepis the same style as their men's, but decorated with gold braid. Some are wearing slouch hats and one officer, sitting on the bottom right of the picture, appears to be wearing a straw hat. Author's collection.

their service in 1862 wearing shapeless long blue coats. 'The exchange to the Zouave uniform from the plain blue infantry uniform was enjoyed immensely,' wrote the 155th's regimental historian. Although they now proudly called themselves Zouaves, the men of the 146th New York were issued with a light blue uniform of the style worn by the *Tirailleurs Algériens* or Turcos of the French army, native North African troops whose record equalled that of the Zouaves. The 146th's trousers lacked quite the same bagginess as Zouave trousers, but the men were happy with their dashing uniforms, which had been manufactured under the personal supervision of their commander, Colonel Kenner Garrard.

Frequently mistaken for Zouaves because of their red trousers, the 14th Regiment New York State Militia, better known by their spectacular title the Red Legged Devils from Brooklyn, were one of a number

of Union militia units whose uniform was inspired by the dress of the *Chasseurs à pied* of the French Army. This smart, comfortable uniform, was adopted by a regimental board of officers in 1860, replacing the 14th's old uniforms that had included blue frock coats.

Some of the 14th's distinctive dark blue jackets had 'false vests' sewn into them. The buttons down the front of the jackets were ornamental and only the vests could be buttoned up, drawing the edges of the jacket closer together. Other types of jackets worn by the 14th didn't have the false vest sewn in at all, but a waistcoat like garment worn under the jacket that fastened at the side and had a line of decorative buttons along the front. Red Austrian knots worn on the shoulders were a prominent feature of 14th Brooklyn jackets early in the war, but many were removed later, possibly because they got in the way and were impractical.

It looked as if the entire Union Army might be dressed in Chasseur uniforms if an experiment outfitting selected infantry regiments in Chasseur dress worked out. In August 1861, Montgomery Meigs the Quartermaster General of the United States Army, sent a letter to the United States embassy in Paris, requesting that the Ambassador order 10,000 complete sets of Chasseur uniforms and equipment for

This 14th Brooklyn private wears the 15 button version of the regiment's jacket which unlike other jackets didn't incorporate a sewn-in false vest. Underneath his jacket this man would wear a Zouave style vest which buttoned up at the side. The buttons down the front of the vest are purely decorative. Martin L. Schoenfeld.

The letters on the forage cap worn by this proud American Chasseur are difficult to make out, but undoubtedly they are the numbers of one of the regiments who were awarded the prize of wearing *Chasseur à pied* uniforms especially imported from France, because of their prowess at drill. This soldier's elaborately plumed full dress shako is just visible on the table beside him. It's often claimed that many of the imported uniforms were too small for strapping American volunteers to wear, but this private fills his uniform comfortably. David Scheinmann.

Union soldiers. The firm of M. Alexis Godillot was contracted to supply the uniforms and accoutrements including French regulation knapsacks and the entire consignment was shipped to New York within four months of the order being placed.

The best regiments in a brigade drill competition held in Fitz John Porter's Division in the Army of the Potomac, were selected to receive the uniforms and the winners were the 62nd Pennsylvania in the 1st Brigade, the 18th Massachusetts in the 2nd Brigade and the 83rd Pennsylvania in the 3rd Brigade. 'Our boys are overjoyed at their good fortune and the colonel says we will have to work hard to keep up our reputation,' wrote one of the uniform recipients in 1861. The Chasseur uniform was the regulation 1860 French light infantry uniform, with a dark blue coat trimmed yellow and ornamented with dark green epaulettes. The full dress cap was leather and a French forage cap was also supplied. Other items included a

fatigue jacket, a hooded jacket known as a *talma*, and white gloves.

The uniform looked spectacular but overall proved to be a disappointment. The average sized Frenchman being smaller than the average American, many of the uniforms proved to be too small, but this problem was alleviated in some cases by putting gussets in the seams. It's debatable whether any complete uniforms were worn in combat, but a soldier of the 83rd at the siege of Yorktown in the summer of 1862 is reported to have had the tassel shot off his cap. Although the 83rd was ordered to put its uniforms into storage in March 1862, it seems some soldiers may have kept 'souvenirs' to wear in the field. Many of the Chasseur uniforms were later 'cannibalised' to provide some of

The popular Chasseur pattern of dress is again reflected in the uniform worn by this young private of the 12th New York State Militia, although the bagginess of his trousers is almost Zouave style. This man wears russet or tan coloured gaiters and his regiment's numbers are visible on the front of his light blue kepi. Mustered in for three months at the beginning of the war, the 12th New York never saw much active service.

David Scheinmann.

the Zouave uniforms for the 155th Pennsylvania. The capes supplied with the uniforms were converted into Zouave jackets and some of the trousers were even converted into Voluminous Zouave pantaloons.

When he originally ordered the uniforms, Quartermaster Meigs wrote that he hoped that they would 'serve as models and will doubtless introduce many improvements in our service,' but he was to be proved wrong. The following year there was a further upsurge in interest in Chasseur uniforms, when it was proposed by a military board that the whole army should be outfitted in them, but the proposal was dropped. It was solely volunteer regiments that brought exotic touches to the Union army.

During the American Civil War, the ethnic background of soldiers was often reflected in the uniforms they wore. Cities teeming with immigrants were full of first or second generation Americans determined to prove their loyalty to their new country, but also anxious not to forget the ties with the military heritage of the places they came from. The 39th New York Volunteers, who were known as the the Garibaldi Guard, were named after the famous Italian patriot and modelled their uniforms on those worn by the famed Italian Light Infantry, the Bersaglieri. The men adopted the famous Bersaglieri hats with a plume of cock feathers and they proudly fixed the initials 'GG' on the front.

The 79th Regiment, New York State Militia was composed largely of men of Scottish ancestry who specifically requested that they be designated the 79th Regiment to establish ties with the British 79th Regiment, the Cameron Highlanders. In the 79th New York's regimental history it was recorded that in October 1860 the men were wearing: 'handsome State jackets with red facings, blue fatigue caps and Cameron tartan pants.'

The men were also later outfitted in kilts for their full dress uniforms. The regiment was mustered into service in early 1861 and had a fine pipe band. But despite being nicknamed the 'Cameron Highlanders' 'Highland Guard' and 'Bannockburn Battalion', it's unlikely that many if any of the 79th wore their kilts or trews at First Bull Run. For some inexplicable reason the men were ordered to lay aside their kilts and trews before the regiment marched into Virginia. Photos later in the war though, do show some members of the 79th in trews and it can be assumed that they were worn on later campaigns.

New York's huge Irish community was represented in the 69th New York State Militia, but romantic tales of the regiment wearing jackets with emerald green cuffs and collars, although mentioned in many accounts about the Civil War, are myth. In 1851 the regiment adopted a green tail coat with a shako but in 1858 when they were designated as an artillery

The 39th New York Volunteers, the famed Garibaldi Guard, parade past President Lincoln. Their authentic copies of the dress worn by the Italian Bersaglieri were some of the most striking uniforms of the war, but on campaign many of the men wore forage caps and red shirts. As shown in this picture, the 39th carried no less than three colours. They not only had the usual national and regimental colours, but carried additional unofficial colours based on the red, white and green design of the Italian National flag. Peter Newark's Military Pictures.

regiment serving as light infantry they wore a New York regulation single breasted dark blue coat.

At First Bull Run many members of the regiment fought in their shirtsleeves and some following Gaelic warrior customs even fought in bare feet. The only really distinctive uniforms worn in the 69th were those worn by Company K who were called the Irish Zouaves or Meagher's Zouaves after their founder, Thomas Francis Meagher, an Irish dissident. Meagher's men wore dark blue jackets and vests trimmed red but their caps and trousers were the same pattern as the rest of the regiment.

The only distinctly Irish part of the uniform was a green waist sash. Company K only wore their colourful uniforms at Bull Run, for the rest of the war they wore standard infantry clothing like their

comrades. At Fredericksburg in 1862, Meagher who now commanded the Irish Brigade of which the 69th became a part, ordered his men to put green sprigs of boxwood in their forage caps to distinguish them from the other Union troops.

There was a bewildering variety of dress in many other militia units on the eve of the war. The Putman Phalanx who were organised in Connecticut in 1858 modelled their uniforms on those worn by the George Washington's Bodyguard during the American Revolution and their dress included tricorne hats. A similar costume was adopted by Ruggles 51st New York State Militia who formed the basis of the 12th New York Infantry, but its doubtful that such antiquarian dress ever saw combat. The Boston Light Infantry who were known as the Tiger Regiment wore black bearskin busbies with a blue plume and gold tassel. Bearskin busbies were a popular feature of many militia units including the Chicago Light Guard, the New York City Guard and the Connecticut Governor's Footguard whose bearskins featured a peak and a resplendent brass cap badge. Many Irish militia regiments criticised the units who wore them, saying that as British Guards units were outfitted with them they were a sign of British oppression. They must have forgotten that the British Army had copied its bearskin

This private of the 79th New York Volunteer Infantry wears the Scottish full dress of his regiment, including a kilt made out of Cameron of Erracht tartan. For undress, tartan trews were also worn, but trying to find supplies of enough tartan to outfit the entire regiment proved to be a problem. On June 2 1861, when the regiment paraded in Baltimore, one journalist reported that the crowd who had come out to see the 79th in their Scottish uniforms was disappointed because only a third of the regiment were outfitted in Scottish dress. Michael J. McAfee.

Colonel Dan Butterfield of the 12th New York State Militia wears his trousers tucked into his gaiters, a habit popular with his entire command. David Scheinmann.

busbies from those worn by Grenadiers in the French Garde Imperiale.

One of the best known American militia units was the Albany Burgesses Corps, formed when leading citizens in Albany petitioned the governor of New York state to form an independent artillery company. The dress coat of the Albany Burgesses Corps was a magnificent scarlet double breasted tailcoat which had

1st Lieutenant Thomas Cartwright wears the regulation uniform of Duryée's Zouaves, the 5th New York Volunteer Infantry. Cartwright died of wounds received at Gaines' Mill in 1862. New York Division of Military and Naval Affairs.

Top right.
Private of the 114th Pennsylvania Volunteer Infantry wears his fez like a skull cap. The cuffs on the 114th's jackets register white or buff in period photos, but they were really light blue in colour. Martin L Schoenfeld.

Right.
The tombeaux designs of the 146th New York Volunteer Infantry show up well in this photograph but like yellow embroidery in most period photographs, they've registered black. This private wears a checked shirt under his jacket. Checked shirts were popular in the Civil War. Martin L. Schoenfeld.

two rows of buttons bearing the letters 'ABC'. Coat tails were turned back and lined white and had a four button pocket flap. Officers wore gold fringed epaulettes with the ABC monogram on the crescent, but apparently the men in the ranks had ones of white worsted.

Line officers and enlisted men wore their black

Lieutenant Colonel Hiram Duryea of the 5th New York flourishes his gaudily decorated kepi. Renowned as a man who could be cool in a crisis he didn't even flinch when a shell came close to exploding underneath his horse during one **battle.** New York Division of Military and Naval Affairs.

Lieutenant W. H. Gurney wears the uniform of the 7th New York State Militia. This picture was taken in Washington in 1861, shortly after the 7th were the first regiment to arrive to 'save the Capital'. David Scheinmann.

bearskin caps for full dress and each bearskin had a gold tassel on the front. Staff officers wore a black full dress chapeau with a black leather plume and gold lace cockade. As an undress uniform the chapeau was replaced with a dark blue cap which had a red and black pompon, held by an elaborate brass ornament bearing the state coat of arms of an embroidered 'NY' within a wreath. In the summer, white linen trousers were worn for parades, otherwise the men wore woollen trousers. The equipment of the Albany Burgesses Corps was equally as sumptuous. Their waistbelts carried a buckle with the initials 'ABC' picked out and their black bayonet scabbards and cartridge boxes were of the finest leather. The Burgesses Corps also had a fatigue uniform which was similar to the regulation United States Army frock coat except the frock coats of the Albany Burgesses Corps were indigo in colour.

The Cincinatti Rover Guards who became part of the 2nd Ohio Volunteer Infantry had an entire dress

uniform made out of scarlet cloth. The coats were trimmed light buff and the trousers had a broad buff stripe on the seam trimmed with gold lace. Caps were regulation but they had a special visor made out of burnished and lacquered leather, richly decorated with a gold embroidered bugle, a star and eagle and the initials CRG. Plumes on the helmets were red tipped white. Cross belts were white and the belt plate for the cross belts was of burnished gilt brass and featured a five pointed star motif. Waistbelts were lacquered, with the initials CRG in burnished metal. The Cincinatti Rover Guards didn't wear its magnificent uniforms all the time. For fatigues, the men wore a less spectacular uniform which had a dark blue jacket, a cap trimmed with red cord and black trousers.

The 22nd Regiment, New York State Militia, was funded by banking and insurance companies in the city who were worried about the departure of so many of New York's militia units who were being posted away to defend Washington. The 22nd New York State Militia wore a grey single breasted frock coat edged with a red collar and cuffs trimmed with white piping. Trousers which were tucked into yellow leather leggings were also grey with a red stripe edged with white piping down the seams. Kepis were grey with a red band and top, which was again edged with white piping. Because of their gaudy trimming the men became known as the Strawberry Greys. For the first year of the war, the 22nd was stationed in New York City but inevitably it was ordered South and was stationed for a time at Harper's Ferry. By this time, though, the regiment had sent home its distinctive grey coats and wore standard regulation army sack coats.

The 1st Regiment Rhode Island Detached Militia wore unusual long blue blouses ending just above the knee, which were not unlike British 18th and 19th century farmers' smocks. The most distinctive part of the regiment's uniform were the rolled red blankets that every man carried. Ambrose E. Burnside, who had organised the regiment and went on to have a particularly disastrous career as a general later in the war, designed the uniforms and according to observers in Washington 'the absence of smart trappings made the unit look ready for business'. Burnside, who seems to have been infinitely better as a tailor than a general, also modified the men's blankets. Each blanket had a hole cut in the centre so that the men could wear them as ponchos and this was particularly welcome in cold weather.

The men of the Second Regiment, New Hampshire Volunteer Militia, began the war wearing 'claw hammer' or 'spiketail' coatees which were almost Napoleonic in style and gave the regiment a particularly distinctive look. Their trousers had a broad red stripe down the seams.

The 71st Regiment New York State Militia elected to wear smart frock coats of the 'national colour' dark blue. The regiment's personnel were native born Americans who saw the increasing number of militia regiments formed from immigrants as a threat. New York's most esteemed militia regiment, the 7th New York State Militia which dated back to 1806, wore a full dress and fatigue uniform both of grey and were

The 75th New York Volunteers had a curious almost nautical style of piping around the cuffs of their jackets, as shown on the jacket of this private. Martin L. Schoenfeld.

known as the 'Old Greybacks'. The fatigue jacket comprised a shorter jacket with black cuffs. The 7th had for a time been commanded by Abram Duryée, who had gone on to found the famed Duryée's Zouaves. Although never seeing combat itself, many of the 7th's officers went on to distinguished careers with other regiments. In Philadelphia the Scott Legion formed from veterans of the Mexican War who had last seen service from 1846 to 1848, wore the regulation Mexican war uniform including sky blue shell jackets and dark blue forage caps.

Regulation Infantry

The blue clad infantryman was the mainstay of Union Forces from 1861-1865. His natural successors were the Doughboys of World War I, the GIs of World War 2 and the Grunts who fought in Vietnam. Orders issued on March 13, 1861, prescribed that the full dress coat for infantrymen should be a dark blue single breasted frock coat made without pleats with a skirt extending one half the distance from the top of the hip to the bend of the knee. The coats were to have nine buttons placed at equal distances on the chest and a stand up collar which shouldn't be too high and restrict a soldier's neck movement. In practice it seems that many collars proved to be uncomfortable and local tailors were often contracted to lower them.

During the war, the Government purchased no fewer than 1,881,727 dress coats which were also worn by many infantrymen in the field. The collar and cuffs for infantry frock coats were piped with blue cord and each cuff had two small brass buttons; one just below the piping, the other above. The regulations also prescribed brass shoulder scales, but these weren't commonly seen on infantrymen's frock coats on campaign.

This line drawing of a Union sack coat shows the practical and comfortable nature of the standard issue garment. Most Civil War soldiers would have worn sack coats at some time during their time of service. Ed Dovey

This is what the typical Union soldier during the Civil War looked like. The private posed against a studio backdrop and not outdoors in camp, wears the standard issue four button sack coat, and an ordinary forage cap. His cartridge box is suspended from a shoulder belt and his belt buckle is the ubiquitous standard 'U.S.' oval model. The only distinguishing points about this soldier are that he hasn't taken care in aligning his belt buckle in the middle of his stomach to look smart for his photo, and the fact that he's turned up the collar on his sack coat. David Scheinmann.

In the field, some men in a regiment might be wearing frock coats, while the rest would be wearing dark blue sack coats. Sack coats evolved from loose fitting fashionable civilian coats of the 1840s which were unusual for the day because they didn't have a seam at the waist, the upper and lower halves being the same piece of cloth.

Sack coats were adopted by the United States Army in 1857 and not only were they cheap to manufacture costing $2.10 each as compared with the $6.56 manufacturing cost for a single frock coat, but they were extremely comfortable to wear and very popular with soldiers throughout the war. Sack coats had no braid or decoration and just a simple turnover collar. Such coats were done up with four large uniform buttons and had an inside pocket on the left breast.

Recruits received sack coats lined with coarse flannel and thin muslin in the sleeves while old sweats wore unlined sack coats. The jackets were produced in four regular sizes; 36 inch breast 30½ leg, 38 inch breast 31½ inch leg, 40 inch breast, 32½ inch leg and 42 inch breast, 33½ inch leg.

From 1858 to 1861 the colour of regular infantry trousers was dark blue but the colour was changed to sky blue on December 16, 1861. Regulation trousers were high in the waist and had full very round legs. Creases in trousers were unknown in those days. Trousers had a modern style button fly and two pockets at the front. Braces attached to buttons on the front and back of the trousers were the universal way of holding them up, belts were not yet much in vogue. Civil War trousers tended to be cut loose and fitted well up over the stomach. A common mistake of many reproduction Civil War trousers worn by re-enactors today is that they hug the hips like modern trousers and the cut, particularly around the crotch, is not baggy enough.

Infantry trousers usually had one inch slits at the bottom to help in getting the straight bottoms over heavy shoes. For size adjustment, a slit was also cut into the back of the trousers at the top and a piece of twine threaded through which could be tied up or loosened. Manufactured in coarse kersey cloth, infantry trousers could cause the men a lot of discomfort, particularly on the march. These lines from a post war medical report about enlisted men published in 1868, are equally applicable to hard marching Civil War soldiers. 'The undeviating thickness of heavy trousers is a source of severe complaint throughout the entire warm season.'

Soldiers were issued with three shirts a year, made in the style of working men's shirts out of flannel, or coarse wool. The army had stopped issuing cotton

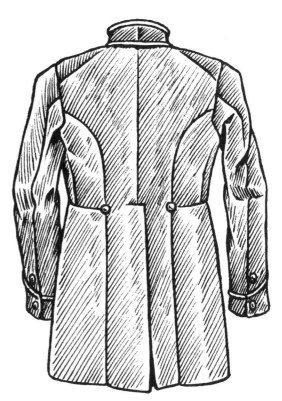

Studying this line drawing of a standard Union issue frock coat, it quickly becomes apparent why many Union soldiers preferred to wear sack coats. Though smart in appearance, frock coats could be uncomfortable to wear, especially with their high collars. Ed Dovey

shirts in 1852, but while flannel shirts may have been warm in winter they were extremly uncomfortable to wear and allegedly more verminous than the many cotton civilian shirts the soldiers wore. Soldiers would try and kill off vermin by smoking their shirts over campfires and crushing them in their fingers was also a popular pastime. Shirts had small turnover collars with a row of three buttons leading up to the neck. They were put on over the head similar to a modern T shirt and were produced in a variety of colours and check designs. Distinctive double breasted firemen's shirts were also popular, often worn as an outer garment over another shirt. Firemen's shirts had wide necks and broad collars, and they were often decorated with bone or mother of pearl buttons. Firemen who enlisted as soldiers, like the Zouaves of the 11th New York Volunteer Infantry, had a particular liking for them.

Although only officially authorised for officers, waistcoats because of their comfort and warmth were worn as a personal choice by all ranks. Usually dark blue in colour, waistcoats had up to four slash pockets on the breast. Soldiers were issued underwear, long drawers stretching to the knee and made of flannel. Some soldiers had never worn underwear before and were baffled by the strange garments. One legendary Civil War story claims that old soldiers told these raw recruits that their drawers were a special parade uniform.

Socks were issued in vast quantities by the Federal government during the Civil War but were not of the highest quality and generally wore out pretty quickly. Many soldiers received pairs of socks as gifts from home and we can easily conjure up a romantic notion of mothers and girlfriends sitting by the fireside, knitting socks for their men far away. Often soldiers used their socks like gaiters and tucked their trousers into them. Gaiters were not a regulation part of the Union uniform and many soldiers found them uncomfortable, but many regiments certainly drew white canvas gaiters from stores, especially Zouave regiments.

Footwear

Ideally infantrymen were supposed to receive four pairs of boots a year. The standard issue were ankle

Infantry private poses with his coat open over his shirt but decorum dictated that his coat should still be buttoned at the collar. Note the height of his kersey trousers coming up well over his waist. His forage cap is standard issue. David Scheinmann.

Cutting a much smarter appearance than many of his comrades in arms, this infantry private has chosen to wear a regulation frock coat and the piping shows up particularly well in the photograph. He looks neat and his brass work is well polished. Just visible behind his feet can be seen the bottom of a stand which photographers stood their subjects against to support them, so that they would not move and blur their images. David Scheinmann.

boots made of leather usually made with the rougher flesh side of the leather on the outside. Soles were sewn to the uppers or fastened by pegs or nails. It appears that the footwear issued, like so many uniforms, could be of dubious quality. Stories of soldiers wearing their boots out with six days of hard marching are not unusual. Army boots were often called brogans and if the sewn soles wore out quickly they were often replaced with pegged soles. For

Infantry private wearing a non-regulation vest under his coat and also a non-regulation bow tie or cravat. Such individual touches were far from unusual. David Scheinmann.

greater comfort, to stop the boots binding round their ankles, soldiers would sometimes cut the tops of their boots down. In the summer some men privately purchased lightweight canvas and leather sporting shoes to wear, which were not unlike modern day bowling shoes.

Private posing without accoutrements in front of a photographer's backdrop, wearing a particularly long looking sack coat which it seems he's somehow endeavoured to tuck up around his waist. David Scheinmann.

Overcoats and ponchos

The U.S. army had been issuing overcoats to its men since 1851. The regulation overcoat was made of sky blue kersey cloth and had a cape that buttoned down the front, but in the clothing rush during the early part of the war, it was not unusual to find men dressed in dark blue and even black overcoats. Infantrymen

In his wrinkled sack coat, this private gives a campaign hardened appearance especially as he's fixed his bayonet to his rifle musket. David Scheinmann.

This infantry private wears a dark blue version of the standard infantryman's overcoat which was usually issued in sky blue. This infantryman's coat is particularly long and he also appears to be wearing a special type of cap, but this is misleading. All he's done is to pin the side badge from his full dress hat to his forage cap, giving an unusual appearance. David Scheinmann.

weren't issued with any wet weather clothing until November 1861, when the Secretary of War authorised the issue of waterproof blankets made out of vulcanised rubber, a technique which had recently been invented. Draped around the shoulders or with a slit cut in them so that they could be slipped over the head, gum blankets provided invaluable protection against the weather and laid down under bedding at night would also help to keep soldiers dry. Soldiers would frequently draw checker boards and other designs on the insides of their blankets making a mobile 'games table'.

Private wearing a regulation overcoat and forage cap but underneath he seems to be dressed in a double breasted fireman's shirt which he's left open at the collar. Such shirts proved to be very popular items of clothing. David Scheinmann.

Standing proud, this infantry corporal wears a frock coat with brass shoulder scales. Largely ornamental, although they could help to deflect a sabre cut, shoulder scales were not widely worn by troops in the field. David Scheinmann.

Headgear

Infantrymen were issued with two types of headgear; a full dress hat and a forage cap. The elaborate full dress hat was adopted in 1858 and named ironically after two future Confederates who had sat on the selection board before the war. The hat was most popularly known as a Hardee hat after Major William J. Hardee

who later became a Confederate general, and sometimes as a Jeff Davis hat, after future Confederate president Jefferson Davis. The origins of the Hardee hat date back to the Mexican war when Colonel Timothy P. Andrews commanding the regiment of Voltigeurs ordered a brimmed hat for his regiment. The war ended before the hats could be worn and they were put in storage until they were discovered by a dragoon captain who issued them to his men.

The 1858 hats were made out of black felt and the three inch brim was looped against the side of the hat and held by a brass 'eagle' fastened to the brim of the crown. The crown of the hat was six inches high and featured the insignia of the particular regiment who were wearing the hats on the front. The most spectacular feature of the hats were the three ostrich feathers fastened to the side and a cord with acorn or tassel designs on the end that encircled the hat. At first the cords were black and yellow and later of various colours. Infantrymen were originally ordered to wear their Hardee hats looped up on the left, but in

It was common for soldiers, particularly in the early stages of the war, to take 'extra' weaponry along with them; especially if the armanent supply to their company or regiment wasn't all that it should be. This infantry private has a Bowie knife stuffed into the front of his shirt, but his huge bow tie looks even more formidable. David Scheinmann.

Photographs showing enlisted men in shirtsleeves are comparatively rare. Note the man's braces and his shirt's baggy sleeves and small collar. This was the most common pattern of shirt found in the Civil War. David Scheinmann.

February 1861 infantrymen were ordered to loop their hats up on the right. The hat cords were originally worn with their tassels on the side opposite the feathers but early in the war there was a vogue for wearing them on the front of the hats.

Despite their pedigree, Hardee hats proved to be unpopular with many infantrymen because they were so stiff and heavy. But some soldiers modified their hats by taking off the elaborate decorations and battering in the crown to make them more comfortable. The most popular headwear of the entire war was the forage cap. The Government made thousands in its factories and purchased many more from contractors. The typical forage cap was made out of dark blue wool backed by an oval sheet of pasteboard to stiffen and shape the top. Forage caps were lined with cotton and the peaks were leather. A number of soldiers had the habit of pushing the peaks up, presumably because they came too far down over

their eyes. Brass buttons held a chin strap in place at the back of the top of the peak but in practice it seems that chin straps weren't often used. Every four years, soldiers were scheduled to receive a black oil cloth forage cap cover as protection in bad weather. Often these cap covers didn't fit properly so men would make their own covers out of their gum blankets.

A popular forage cap accessory in the early part of the Civil War was the havelock, a piece of cloth fitted over the top of the forage cap and sometimes over the peak as well, that draped down over a soldier's neck for protection against the sun. Havelocks were named after British general Sir Henry Havelock and first worn by British troops in the scorching heat during the Indian Mutiny. Havelocks for the entire 69th New York were provided by a group of patriotic New York ladies at the beginning of the war but later their fascination waned and many were used as bandages or for straining coffee. By the later war period no havelocks were in use.

The 42nd Pennsylvania Volunteer Infantry

A Union soldier at the re-enactment of First Bull Run in 1995, at Weston Park, Shropshire, is pictured wearing a havelock over his forage cap. In theory, the cloth covers were meant to deflect the heat, but many soldiers found the cloth flapping around their heads uncomfortable, especially under battlefield conditions. Ron Field.

Regiment, largely lumbermen from the tough wild cat regions of Pennsylvania, had a unique way of decorating their forage caps. Each soldier of the regiment sported a strip of deerhide on his forage cap and the regiment become known as the Bucktails. Tradition has it that James Landregan of Company I was the first to put a bucktail in his cap and the rest of the regiment quickly followed suit, Bucktails were eventually adopted by an entire Bucktail Brigade formed in 1862 from the 149th and 150th Pennsylvania Infantry. The Pennsylvania originators of the Bucktail tradition sneered at these upstarts, calling them 'bogus Bucktails'.

Although never as popular as standard issue forage caps, McClellan caps were also worn by Union soldiers. These caps were of the French Chasseur pattern and with lower sides than typical forage caps, they were more of a French kepi style. The McClellan caps were popular with several Zouave regiments, like the 72nd Pennsylvania who wore McClellan caps with red piping around the crowns. High crowned forage caps were popular with some men because they could slip a sponge, hankerchief or leaves underneath as protection against the sun. Some enterprising sutlers also sold the men forage cap ventilators; pieces of brass gauze which could be pushed into the top of a forage cap to help the air circulate over the wearer's head.

Broad brimmed slouch hats were sometimes worn by the soldiers in Eastern regiments but slouch hats were more popular with Western regiments, who effected more of a rugged appearance than their Eastern counterparts. Private Rice Bull of the 123rd New York Infantry wrote: 'Western troops looked quite unlike our men. They all wore large hats instead of caps.' Straw hats were also popular in certain regiments and must have provided much relief against the sun, but they had their disadvantages. Straw hats were issued to the entire 16th New York in 1862, but the men found their unusual headgear made them easy targets and they were quickly discarded in favour of forage caps.

Union Infantry Equipment

Since the days of the American Revolution, American

Standing like the Emperor Napoleon, with hand in coat, was a popular pose for many Civil War soldiers having their photographs taken. This soldier stands almost completely accoutred and the top of his bayonet in its scabbard can just be seen, but he appears to lack a cartridge box. David Scheinmann.

Oil cloths were practical forage cap accessories in bad weather. This private has slipped an oil cloth over his forage cap and poses for this picture wearing a standard issue frock coat. David Scheinmann.

soldiers liked to travel light. This may have had a lot to do with the shortages of supply that dogged America during the struggle for independence, but also with the American volunteers' attitude to authority. An American soldier believed he was fighting for a cause and prided himself on his individuality. He considered excess equipment unnecessary and this was reflected in the design of the accoutrements issued to him and the way he would discard anything he found uncomfortable; although in this respect the Union soldier was not as undisciplined as his Confederate foes.

Non-commissioned officers were authorised to wear dark blue stripes down the seams of their trousers, one and half inches wide. In practice many sergeants and corporals didn't bother, possibly because their trousers didn't come ready made with the stripes and sewing them on was too much trouble. This corporal though, is proud to show off his stripes and he is also wearing a fine looking waistcoat. David Scheinmann.

This studio portrait of a sergeant offers a far more realistic view of how Civil War soldiers actually looked. Note his hat is probably cut down and battered into shape from a full dress Hardee hat. David Scheinmann.

The basic equipment issued to all Union infantry soldiers included a knapsack worn on the back and a cartridge box which was either suspended on a belt over the left shoulder or carried on a waistbelt which also carried the soldier's bayonet and cap pouch. Waistbelts were 1.9 inches wide and 38.5 inches long and they were usually buckled with a brass waistbelt plate with US on the front. Variations included the popular SNY plates standing for State of New York favoured by many New York volunteers. Confederates joked that SNY stood for 'snotty nosed Yank'. Other variations in waist belt plates worn by troops from various states included NHSM plates sported by men of the New Hampshire State Militia. Infantry shoulder belt plates were 2½ inches in diameter. Completing his basic equipment, the Union infantryman carried a haversack and canteen slung over his right shoulder.

Knapsacks

There were two main types of knapsacks; rigid and non-rigid. Rigid knapsacks were particularly favoured by militia units in the early stages of the war and had a square wooden frame covered with waterproof cloth or canvas with two small straps on top to secure a blanket. These rigid knapsacks looked full whether anything was in them or not, adding to a regiment's neat appearance on the parade ground. In the Mexican War, American infantry had worn a rigid knapsack with a waterproofed cover. Though looking smart, rigid knapsacks could be uncomfortable to wear.

In 1853 a non-rigid model knapsack was

Opposite.
Standing by a stack of arms and a typically ornate drum, the sergeant major is fully clothed and equipped and carries a regulation sword. This image is one of a contemporary series of photographs made to demonstrate the dress of the various Union services. Few soldiers would have looked as ideal as this on campaign. David Scheinmann.

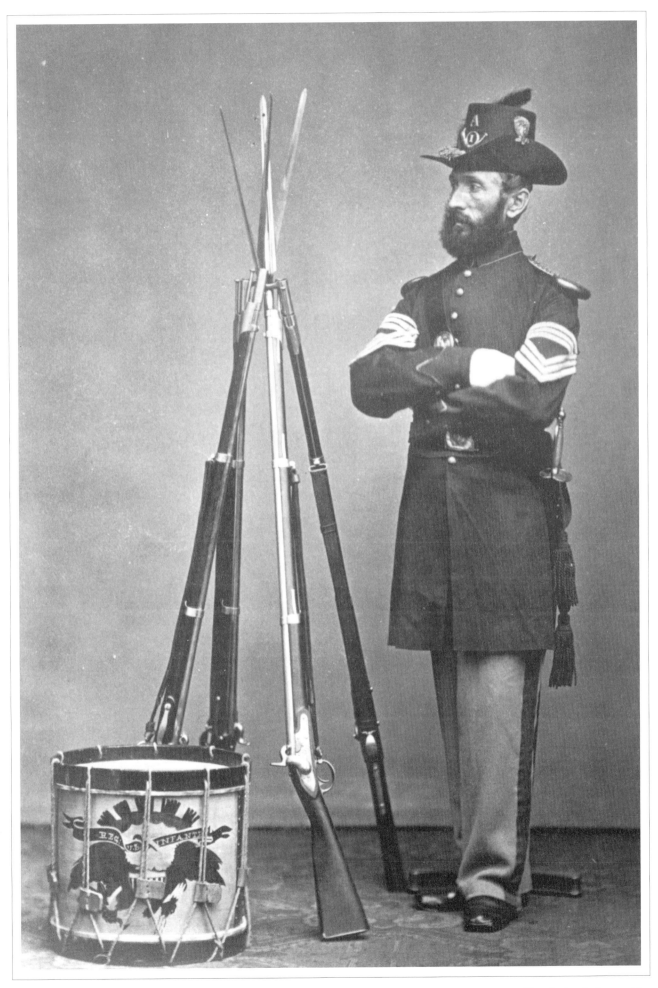

introduced, but it seems the majority of militia units were content to remain with the old rigid model. Knapsacks covered in animal hide which were favoured in Europe were quite rare in America. But they had been part of the consignment of Chasseur uniforms ordered by the United States government and Berdan's Sharpshooters were also issued with them.

'Soft' knapsacks of waterproofed cotton or canvas were the knapsacks most often carried by infantry soldiers in the Civil War. In 1857 army regulations ordered that all knapsacks should be painted black. Infantry knapsacks were to carry their owner's regimental number in the centre and officially this number was to be one and a half inches in length and painted in white paint. Knapsacks were also to be marked on the inside with the letter of the company the soldier belonged to.

Many soldiers dispensed with knapsacks or lost them on campaign. The 5th New York, whose original

14th Brooklyn re-enactors relaxing in camp display the type of stiff knapsacks that were a favourite with militia units in the early war years. The 14th kept their smart red blankets rolled on top and the regimental numerals are stencilled on the backs of their knapsacks, a common practice with many Civil War regiments. Robert C. Duffy.

knapsacks had been manufactured by the Gutta Percha Company of New York, lost many of theirs after the battle of Malvern Hill. No rules seem to have been enforced about knapsacks and for comfort, many soldiers particularly infantrymen in the Western campaigns, tossed their knapsacks aside, preferring instead to keep their belongings in a blanket roll tied around the shoulders. This romantic image of soldiers with their possessions bundled up in a blanket is usually associated with Confederates, but it was a common practice with Union soldiers as well. A knapsack crammed full of blankets and personal items could easily become unbearable on the march, especially with the sun heating up the waterproofed canvas. A blanket roll draped around the body was much easier to march with.

Cartridge boxes and cap pouches

The standard infantry cartridge box was made out of black leather and contained two tin inserts each with an upper and lower section where infantrymen kept 40 black powder cartridges. Many infantrymen kept extra cartridges in their coat pockets, transferring them to their cartridge boxes, especially when the supply in the cartridge box containers ran out. Cartridge boxes could be suspended on a soldier's waist belt, but a well stocked cartridge box weighs over three pounds, so it

Veterans of the 7th Illinois Infantry all wore frock coats to pose for this picture, except for the sergeant on the far left. They are all armed with formidable Henry repeating rifles, the forerunner of the Winchester; and it's a rarity to find Civil War infantrymen so well equipped. It could be that the soldiers privately purchased the weapons they so proudly hold. Peter Newark's Military Pictures.

made more sense to carry the box on a shoulder belt and distribute the weight more easily. Regulation cap pouches were of black leather and were lined with sheepskin. The corners of the outer flaps fitted tightly over a brass stud and were rounded at the edges.

Haversacks and canteens

Haversacks and canteens were the fundamental items of equipment which kept the Union soldier alive. In his haversack he stored his food and eating utensils. Rations included salt pork, sugar, coffee, salt and the staple diet of all Civil War soldiers, hard tack, a biscuit made out of flour mixed with water which was then baked. It was so hard it never rotted and it was not unknown for hardtack to be issued to soldiers long after the Civil War had ended. Eating utensils would usually comprise a knife, fork, spoon and tin plate, but some soldiers even carried non-regulation fancy mess

tins. All soldiers had a tin cup which they sometimes carried on the outside of their haversacks looped through the strap.

The regulation haversack was made out of waterproofed cotton cloth. It had a single strap with a buckle, and inside there was a removable cotton bag held in place by three buttons. On a hot day one can imagine what the effect on the contents of this bag would be. Heat exhaustion and not battle was often the cause of many soldiers dying. The sides of roads where the troops passed, would often be lined with soldiers who simply had become victims of the blazing weather conditions and the excessive humidity, which characterised the Civil War campaigning season throughout the United States.

At Gettysburg, soldiers from both sides are said to have shared water from the same source of supply at Spangler's Spring. The regulation canteen 1858 pattern held almost three pints of water and was made out of two convex pieces of tin soldered together. It had a cork stopper and was covered in blue or brownish woollen cloth.

It is usually accepted that blue was the standard colour for canteen covers, but it actually seems likely that brown was the most common colour. In theory the covers kept the contents cool and helped to stop the canteens making a noise on the march, but many soldiers had canteens without covers.

After 1861 rings were pressed into both sides of metal canteens and this 'bullseye' type of canteen became the classic canteen of the Civil War, but there were many varieties of canteen including cylindrical wooden canteens and even canteens made out of leather. Soldiers often personalised their canteens by painting their name and company number on the cloth cover or by carving their initials and company number on wooden canteens.

Infantry Weapons

The basic arm of the Union infantry soldier during the American Civil War was a muzzle loading rifle musket and troops were armed with a bewildering variety of these weapons. Not only was there a scramble to get troops uniformed at the beginning of

Typical Union haversack in which soldiers kept their food and other essential requirements. The haversacks had a detachable inner lining shown on the right of the picture which could be taken out and washed. If the soldier was carrying salted pork or other forms of meat as part of his rations in hot weather, this was very necessary, although as plenty of accounts of the time reveal, many soldiers didn't bother to be so fastidious with their haversacks. Ed Dovey.

the war, there was also a panic to get recruits armed. The situation wasn't helped by the fact that the Confederates had captured Federal arsenals in South Carolina, Louisiana, and Texas, and at Harper's Ferry, Virginia. The total number of muskets available to Union soldiers looked fine on paper and numbered over 437,000, but less than 40,000 of these pieces were serviceable modern weapons. The majority were antique pieces that had been altered from flintlock to the percussion system.

The first 'modern' weapon used by Union troops was the 1855 rifle musket designed to take a Minie ball of the type invented in France to make loading rifled weapons easier. The rifle also used the Maynard percussion system which worked rather like a child's toy cap gun. Instead of placing a metal percussion cap on the nipple of the gun to fire the charge in the barrel, a mechanism rolled out a line of paper percussion caps each time the weapon was cocked.

The Springfield rifle musket, developed from the 1855 rifle musket which was expensive to produce, is the weapon most closely associated with American infantrymen and these weapons became the workhorse of Union forces in the Civil War. The Springfield Armoury in Massachusetts began turning out massive quantities of the rifles in 1861.

Both the Union and the Confederacy despatched

Regulations regarding facial hair during the American Civil War stated that beards should be kept trim and neat, but these rules were often ignored, which accounts for the spectacular beards sported by many officers and men. Goatees and moustaches were generally favoured by officers, although this officer has gone to extremes. He wears a regulation frock coat with a single row of nine buttons down the front, marking him out as a company officer. David Scheinmann.

A good view of the regulation waist sash worn by first sergeants. They were made out of red worsted material, with bullion fringed ends, meant to hang down no more than 18 inches from where the sash was tied on the left hip. Regulations stated that sashes were to be worn on all occasions apart from fatigue duties, but they were rarely seen on campaign. David Scheinmann.

agents to Europe to procure arms to supplement domestically produced weapons. Many rifles were imported from Germany and France but the most

serviceable and popular imported rifle muskets were British Enfield rifle muskets. By the middle of the war it was estimated that half of the Union troops were armed with Enfields and what made this weapon

Infantry officer in full dress complete with epaulettes and white gauntlets. It's likely that ostentatious officers may have worn epaulettes on campaign, but in the majority of cases they were replaced by ordinary shoulder straps. David Scheinmann.

Officers' waist sashes were fabricated out of crimson silk net but differed little from those worn by sergeants. This infantry officer also wears an expensive looking forage cap, its high crown perhaps marking it out as a McDowell pattern forage cap. David Scheinmann.

particularly popular was that its calibre was almost identical to the domestically produced Springfield rifle musket. The same ammunition could be used for both weapons.

The method of loading a weapon hadn't changed dramatically since Napoleonic times. Soldiers still tore open cartridges and rammed home the charge; but unlike old flintlocks there were no priming pans on their rifles, the percussion system was much more efficient, particularly in wet weather. In many regiments soldiers found themselves with different weapons. In one company of a Pennsyslvania regiment

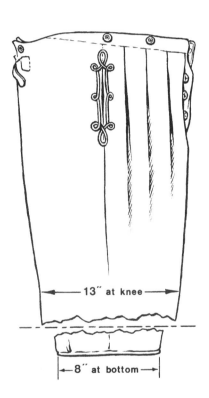

the majority had Enfield and Springfield muskets mixed with soldiers who carried Belgian and Austrian rifle muskets.

When it was mustered in, the 5th New York was armed with a mixture of weapons including Harper's Ferry muskets and muskets converted to the percussion system with locks dated 1844 and 1845. The regiment didn't exchange all its smoothbores for Springfield rifles until May 1862.

Thomas Meagher, who raised the Irish Zouaves, Company K 69th New York, and who later commanded the Irish Brigade in the Union Army,

The elaborate details of a privately purchased Zouave officer's uniform are shown here in a line drawing of the dress worn by Captain Felix Agnus of the 165th New York Volunteer Infantry. The trousers were a rust red colour trimmed in gold and the dark blue jacket featured yet more elaborate ornamentation. The false vest sewn into the jacket and held in place with flaps and buttons over the left shoulder, was decorated with ornate tombeaux designs, not visible in this picture. The Z in the regulation bugle horn motif worn on the front of Agnus' kepi was a common feature of Zouave officers' headwear. Ed Dovey.

Bandsmen were important for morale and usually wore a more ornate version of standard infantry dress. These are men of the 12th Indiana Volunteer Infantry wearing the semi Zouave dress of the regiment. In battle, bandsmen acted as stretcher bearers. Michael J. McAfee.

wanted all his men to be armed with model 1842 smoothbore muskets. In theory, rifle muskets could be used at longer ranges because they were more accurate, but Meagher thought that having his men armed with less accurate smoothbore muskets would suit the close quarters fighting at which he wanted his men to excell and emulate their ancestors. But the truth is that although rifle muskets were more accurate than smoothbores their increased range was often negated by the tremendous amount of black powder smoke. In general soldiers could only see for short distances through this smoke, so the advantages of a rifled musket were often literally blotted out.

The effects can be appreciated by spectators at modern day Civil War re-enactments where even comparatively small amounts of men firing muzzleloading weapons quickly become shrouded in black powder smoke.

Breech-loading weapons were available in the Civil War, but were mainly confined to use by the cavalry. It

was thought that if breech loading weapons were used by standard infantrymen then they would waste ammunition. However breech-loading weapons did see use with the infantry notably with the 42nd Pennsylvania and Berdan's Sharpshooters who used Sharps carbines. The Sharps carbine had a sliding breechlock which was opened by pulling the trigger guard down. A linen cartridge was inserted in the breech and when the breechlock was closed the back of the cartridge was sheered off. Sharps carbines had a percussion lock but a magazine held a number of detonating pellets which were ejected on to the nipple. An interesting feature of Sharps carbines was that some models incorporated a small coffee mill with a detachable handle in the butt.

Colt who were chiefly renowned for pistols, produced a rifle with a revolving chamber. It was the first repeating rifle adopted by the United States Government and early models had been used in the Seminole War in 1838, but there was a considerable sideflash when the weapon was fired and also the danger that all six cylinders would go off at once. The rifle saw limited use in the war; Berdan's Sharpshooters used them while they were waiting to be armed with Sharps rifles. In their formidable armoury, Berdan's Sharpshooters also had a variety of

A lieutenant of the 18th United States Coloured Troops wears a broad brimmed slouch hat and a waistcoat under his frock coat. David Scheinmann.

This comfortably dressed officer wears a sack coat with a narrow cut. This sack coat does not appear to have any shoulder straps, but he wears an officer's sash underneath his waistbelt. David Scheinmann.

specialist sniper rifles many of which had been privately purchased.

The most sought after breechloading weapon of the Civil War was the Spencer carbine. A tube in the stock fed copper cased bullets into the breech. Southern soldiers said that Northerners could load up their Spencers on Sundays and fire them all week. Captured Spencers were highly prized, but the South lacked the capability of making ammunition for them. When stocks of captured ammunition were exhausted, they couldn't be used.

Bayonets

Socket bayonets were used with both Enfield and Springfield rifle muskets. 18 inches long and with 3 inch sockets they fitted snugly over the top of the musket barrel latched on to the top sight. Bayonet scabbards were made out of leather and capped in brass. A black buff leather frog sewn and rivetted together was attached to the scabbard and suspended from the waist belt at an angle. Bayonet scabbards were worn under the soldier's haversack and canteen.

Union Infantry Officers' Dress

Officially all infantry officers in regulation dress were to wear frock coats of dark blue cloth. These coats had a standing collar usually about $1\frac{1}{2}$ inches in height and reached down two thirds to three fourths of the distance from the top of the hip to (continued on p. 56)

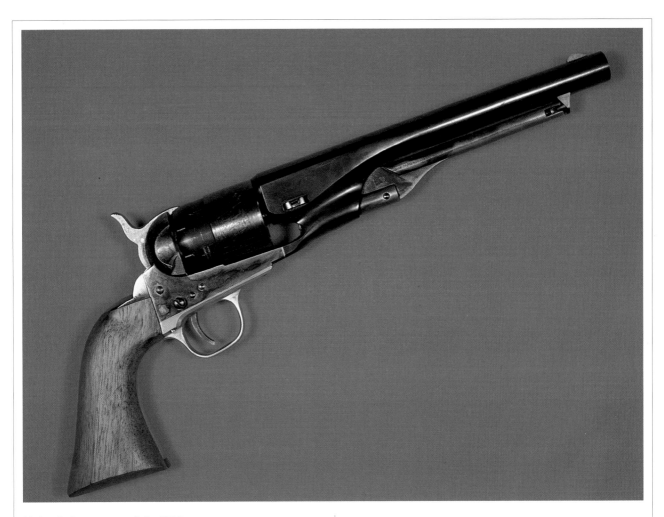

Union Infantryman, July 1863.

Although the American Civil War saw the creation of many exotically clad regiments, the Union private depicted here is a typical foot soldier of the Union Army. He carries a knapsack with his blanket neatly stowed on top. Northern mills couldn't manufacture enough supplies of wool for standard Army issue blankets, so lightweight blankets were distributed, made out of a woollen and cloth mixture.

Army blankets had the letters 'US' crudely stiched into them and they also had black stripes at each end. Blankets were large enough for the average soldier to curl up in, but the warmth value of many blankets was negligible. Of far more worth would be the single rubber blanket that each soldier carried in his knapsack. Spread on the ground it would keep him reasonably dry at night. Soldiers also carried a canvas shelter half in their knapsacks which when buttoned together with a comrade's shelter half and secured over a wooden frame, usually the locally cut branches of a tree, made a small tent as illustrated in this picture. Called shelter halves or dog tents, they were extremely uncomfortable for two or even sometimes three soldiers to sleep in. Shelter halves were narrow and short and often leaked badly; but they were 'home' to many soldiers.

The soldier's forage cap is regulation and has a 5th Corps badge sewn on top. A distinctive forage cap variation; the McDowell pattern with its high crown, is also illustrated.

The private wears a standard four button sack coat and sky blue regulation trousers, long in the leg on this soldier. Many men tucked their trousers into their heavy woollen socks, making a crude form of gaiters. Shoes were often hobnailed as illustrated, but even then heavy marching could quickly reduce a pair of shoes to shreds very quickly.

This soldier keeps his tin cup suspended from the chain of his canteen, a practice with some infantrymen. Many canteen straps and haversack straps were too long, so soldiers would shorten the straps by knotting them.

By the time of Gettysburg, arms in the Union Army had become more standardised. There was still an odd mixture of domestic and imported weapons, but many soldiers were armed with a Springfield rifle musket like the one illustrated here. Bayonets played their part in combat throughout the Civil War, most memorably during the charge by the 20th Maine at Gettysburg. Painting by Chris Collingwood.

Above.
Colt firearms provided many pistols to the cavalry before and during the Civil War. This is a Colt .44 Army model 1860, a leading cavalry weapon of the Civil War. Peter Newark's Military Pictures.

The officer in this picture holds a kepi decorated with gold braid and it's likely that he is a Zouave or Chasseur officer. Despite the gaudy dress of their men, many of these officers wore standard frock coats and one of the loops to support the waist belt can be seen on this officer's coat. David Scheinmann.

Thomas Callan was a lieutenant in the 128th United States Coloured Troops whose officers and men took a particular pride in their appearance. Not only did they have to face the enemy, but also prejudice about the worth of coloured troops from their own side. All officers of coloured troops were white and most were staunch abolitionists. Many black troops serving under officers like Callan preferred wearing frock coats in the field and their clothing was standard infantry issue. Some black troops were outfitted in red trousers but these were later rejected because the men didn't want to be set apart from white troops. David Scheinmann.

frockcoats had been getting fuller. Sleeves were generally 17 inches wide in 1861 and some officers wore them 20 inches wide before the war ended.

For full dress, officers wore gilt epaulettes with a sky blue disc set on the crescent with the regimental number embroidered on the disc in gold. Rank badges were displayed on the epaulette strap. Colonels had a

the bottom of the knee. Coats were double breasted for colonels and single breasted for captains and lieutenants. Colonels' coats had two rows of seven buttons on the chest, while captains' and lieutenants' coats had one row of nine buttons on the chest, placed at equal distances. Since 1851 the sleeves of officers'

Opposite.
The collar of this officer's jacket appears to be lined in black velvet. His regiment isn't known, but judging by the bagginess of his trousers and the amount of ornamentation on his sleeves he was an officer in a Zouave or Chasseur regiment. David Scheinmann.

Neatly turned out Union infantryman with a watch chain hanging from his non-regulation waistcoat. The majority of Union soldiers liked to adapt uniforms to suit themselves. David Scheinmann.

This company officer wears regulation dress. Despite the habit of many officers of wearing various forms of clothing, this is what a typical officer, perhaps without his waist sash, would have looked like in the field. David Scheinmann.

silver eagle, captains had two silver bars while lieutenants had one silver bar. On campaign, officers wore shoulder straps, embroidered in gold around the edges with rank insignia displayed on each end.

Like their frock coats, infantry officers' trousers were made of a finer material than those of enlisted men. Regulations of 1861 stated that they should be of

Opposite.
An infantry company officer poses with the regimental colour of his regiment. Union regiments carried two colours into battle, the national colour and the regimental colour. Some became so worn in combat that little more remained of them than shreds and they had to be 'retired'. David Scheinmann.

Posed against a painted background this officer is wearing white gloves and the detail of his waist sash shows up well. With his style of hair and beard, he looks very 'old school'. David Scheinmann.

Well groomed infantry officer wearing regulation frock coat and forage cap. David Scheinmann.

dark blue cloth with a sky blue welt, one eighth of an inch in diameter, let into the outer seam. Officers were authorised to wear ties or cravats, but regulations stated that the tie was not to be visible at the opening of the collar.

Custom dictated that an officer should not show his shirt front, waistcoats worn under the frock coat were extremely useful for covering up the officer's shirt when he opened his frockcoat for comfort in the hot weather.

Commissioned officers wore a cloak coat of dark blue cloth closed by four frog buttons made out of black silk and loops of black silk cord. Rank was indicated on both sleeves by a knot of black silk braid. A colonel's coat had five braids in a single knot and a captain's had two braids in a single knot.

Union officers, like officers in all armies, enjoyed considerable freedom of dress. In the field they often discarded their frock coats in favour of short jackets and loose fitting sack coats, which were longer and shouldn't be confused with enlisted men's sack coats.

Some officers even left off the authorised shoulder straps on their sack coats so that they would be less conspicuous in the field, but this was not common practice. Since they were not regulation, officer's sack coats came in a variety of styles. The most common was a four button coat made out of flannel, while a style favoured with New York officers was of dark blue cloth with five buttons and pockets on either side in the front. These pockets, together with the fronts, collars and bottom edges of the coats, were edged in half inch black mohair braid. Some officers' sack coats were even made with comfortable velvet collars, to provide maxiumum comfort to the wearer on campaign.

The dress of officers commanding the many militia regiments in the Union forces, provided variations on the regulation officers' uniforms. In 1861 officers of the 11th New York Volunteer Infantry wore grey double breasted frock coats with two rows of seven buttons on the chest and four small buttons set on gold braid loops on the cuff slashes. Shoulder straps

A typical Union soldier has his image taken with his wife. Judging by the man's war weary demeanour, it was taken during a period of leave. David Scheinmann.

were dark blue with a red edging and the officer's trousers were also grey with gold stripes down the seams edged in red. Captain J. Blake of the 69th New York State Militia wore a short jacket edged in gold and black braid. The jacket also had gold shoulder knots. Completing the uniform, Blake's trousers were dark blue edged with gold stripes down the seams. Not only did Thomas Francis Meagher wear a gold trimmed Zouave uniform when he formed Company K of the 69th New York, at Fredericksburg in December 1862, he was reported to have worn a frock coat made out of green velvet. Colonel Robert Nugent of the 69th, was renowned for wearing a checked shirt under his jacket and an officer's black and gold hat cord as a neck tie.

As might be expected, the uniforms worn by Union Zouave officers were extremely colourful. Minutes of a meeting held by 5th New York officers on April 27 1861 prescribed that the trousers should be 'red and large no stripe'. Officers also wore smart dark blue frock coats for full dress, but their fatigue uniforms were a matter of personal choice. One officer, Captain

The picture of this infantry officer demonstrates the way swords were carried, hooked up comfortably on the waistbelt. David Scheinmann.

Cleveland Winslow, was particularly spectacular in his mode of dress. Zouave Thomas Southwick wrote: 'Instead of a military frock coat which was part of the uniform worn by other officers, he wore a fancy Zouave jacket gaudily decorated. His military cap he jauntily wore on one side of his head. Altogether he was half Italian bandit and half English highwayman, a romantic looking fellow.'

This infantry officer wears a short fatigue jacket. Many officers designed such jackets to their own specifications. David Scheinmann.

The uniform of Felix Agnus who commanded the 165th New York, Second Battalion Duryée Zouaves, was equally as spectacular. Tailored by Brooks Brothers of New York, the jacket was decorated with red tape and cord offset with gilt cord. The jacket sleeves had galloons of two intertwined strips of gold braid and each sleeve opening from cuff to shoulder was decorated with 10 brass ball buttons.

Lieutenant William M. Wells of the 56th Pennsylvania Volunteer Infantry Regiment wears a long four button officer's sack coat. His hat is a cut down Hardee hat with all the insignia removed. David Scheinmann.

Officer's headwear

Many officers wore kepis which were similar in style to forage caps but were lower and had a straight visor. The tops of the kepis were also countersunk and had a rim. Tops of the kepis worn by Zouave and Chasseur officers would usually feature much gold trimming. McClellan style kepis favoured by many officers featured a square ducktail brim. Officers also wore forage caps, and the distinctive McDowell style of forage cap was particularly high in the crown. Some officers' kepis and forage caps were lined with silk. Hardee hats were regulation headwear for both officers and men; but like the soldiers, many officers found them uncomfortable to wear preferring wide brimmed slouch hats in the field.

Officer's weapons

All officers carried swords, but they were rarely used in combat and were worn more as a badge of rank. The regulation staff and field officers' swords were the

1850 pattern, carrying the initials US in the floral designs on the brass guard. Many variations of these swords were made abroad particularly in Klingenthal, Germany. The 1860 pattern sword had a graceful thin blade but failed to carry much favour with officers, who preferred the sturdier 1858 pattern. Swords, mainly the 1840 non-commissioned officer's sword were also carried by sergeants throughout the Civil War and were in service with the American army as late as 1910.

Pistols

Surprisingly, handguns were not part of the official arms issue to infantry officers. Sidearms carried by infantry officers and indeed the many infantrymen who began the war with a brace of pistols stuck into their belts, were privately purchased. The most common sidearm was the famous Colt six shot single action revolver. Each cylinder in the revolver was loaded using a paper or linen cartridge containing powder and ball rammed home with a rammer under the barrel. A percussion cap was then placed on the nipple at the other end of the chamber and each time the hammer was cocked, the cylinder was rotated and fired when the trigger was pulled and the hammer hit the cap.

Some soldiers, like the man in this picture, had the curious habit of tilting their kepis up. It wasn't merely fashionable, but a practical way of keeping sweat out of a soldier's eyes. David Scheinmann.

Cavalry and Artillery

On the eve of the Civil War, the cavalry arm of the Union forces, like the infantry, was woefully understrength. There were only five regiments of regular cavalry and they were out protecting settlers on the plains. The 1st Regiment of dragoons had been recruited in 1836 while the 2nd regiment had originally been raised as a mounted rifle regiment in 1844. The 1st and 2nd Cavalry, the newest of these regiments, had been raised in 1855. A third cavalry regiment was raised in June 1861 and later all the regular mounted units were redesignated as the 1st, 2nd, 3rd, 4th and 5th cavalry regiments in order of seniority.

The army could also draw on the small number of mounted militia units in the North, but these were never as many as the infantry militia units. Maintaining horses and equipment was expensive in the North which unlike the rural South did not have such fine traditions of horsemanship. Nevertheless some militia cavalry units had flourished in the North. The 3rd Regiment, Hussars, of the New York State Militia, wore dark blue cloth jackets and fur busbies but it was said that their horses were delivery wagon horses, used by many of the regiment's personnel in their ordinary jobs. As a whole, the regiment didn't see action during the Civil War but one troop was in service with the Army.

The National Lancers of Boston whose lineage dated back to 1836 and who became Troop A of the 1st Battalion of Light Dragoons, Massachussetts Volunteer Militia wore smart red jackets and elaborate czapkas as part of their full dress uniform. Men from the National Lancers, minus their lances, saw service with the 1st Massachusetts Volunteer Cavalry and anybody experienced on a horse was a boon to the struggling Union cavalry.

General Winfield Scott, the ageing War of 1812 and Mexican War hero, who commanded the United States Army at the outbreak of the Civil War, had cantankerously spurned the use of cavalry for the coming struggle and many offers from established militia regiments or offers to raise fresh regiments were rejected by the War Department. A diehard artilleryman, Scott maintained that the war would be decided by cannon and that Northern cavalrymen would not be able to operate properly in the South. Volunteer cavalry was accepted on the basis that individual states provided mounts and equipment.

The North was slow in recruiting cavalry. A request to raise a serious number of 40,000 cavalry was not made until February 1862, when each state was asked to supply cavalry units. Equipment shortages which had also plagued the infantry were prevalent. At the beginning of the war the government had barely 5,000 sets of horse equipment to issue. Outfitting a cavalry regiment was also very expensive, costing in excess of $400,000. However there were advantages to recruiting a cavalry regiment.

Cavalry had always been the most glamorous arm of military service as they swept passed lowly infantrymen, so recruiting usually went well among men who wanted to be something more than a foot soldier. The trouble was that the men who knew horses well, such as farmers, also knew the amount of work in caring for a horse and enlisted elsewhere. Quite often, eager recruits were city boys with no real knowledge of the animals; but they soon learned. Even before he was taught the most basic drill moves, the cavalryman was taught how to look after his mount.

Despite the government's extra investment in equipping the cavalry, it was not used as decisively as Confederate cavalry in the early stages of the war. Union cavalry was largely confined to picket duty

Opposite.
Charles H. Masland of the 6th Pennsylvania Cavalry, the famous Rush's Lancers, draws his sword for a patriotic pose. Note the shoulder scales on Masland's uniform which the Lancers favoured more than other cavalry regiments.
USAAMHI/Jim Enos.

Union cavalryman in shell jacket with shoulder scales. He's also wearing dark blue trousers undoubtedly reinforced on the insides of the legs to cope with the rigours of being on horseback. David Scheinmann.

A cavalryman stands beside his horse, wearing a pair of gauntlets which surprisingly were not standard issue for mounted troops and had to be privately purchased. David Scheinmann.

resulting in the frequent infantryman's jibe 'Whoever saw a dead cavalryman?' Eventually the cavalry gained its independence and grouped into brigades and divisions became equal to Southern horsemen.

Cavalry Dress

Officially, cavalrymen were to wear a short jacket usually called a shell jacket made out of of dark blue cloth, with one row of 12 small eagle buttons on the the chest placed at equal distances. The stand up collar was cut away at an angle of 30 degrees and had two blind buttonholes on each side in yellow worsted three eighths of an inch wide, each with one small button. The top buttonhole was four inches long, the lower three and a half inches long. The bottom and front ends of the collar were edged in the same braids, as were the front edge, bottom and two back seams of the coat. Yellow was the facing cover for cavalry, but the 1st and 2nd cavalry who had been mustered into service as the 1st and 2nd dragoons before the Civil War, were proud of their heritage and some of their jackets were lined in orange, the dragoons' traditional facing colour.

To hold his waist belt in place, the cavalryman had two small bolsters stitched to the back of his jacket. Shorter and more stylish than the infantryman's standard sack coat, the tight fitting shell jackets which extended only as far as the cavalryman's waist gave him

Private pictured wearing the regulation double breasted overcoat for mounted men, but the coat has far fewer buttons on the cape than are normally seen. Wearing coats like these when mounted, could be warm but cumbersome. David Scheinmann.

greater ease when moving in the saddle, but nevertheless cavalrymen would wear sack coats or fatigue blouses in the field. These fatigue blouses reached halfway down the thigh and were made out of dark blue flannel. They fastened with four brass buttons and like a sack coat had an inside pocket over the left breast. Like infantryman's trousers, cavalry trousers were standard issue blue kerseys but they were reinforced around the crotch and inside legs to prevent wear.

Cavalrymen were issued with sky blue cloth overcoats similar to those of the infantry. They had a stand up collar five inches high and were double breasted with two rows of buttons. The coats fell to six to eight inches below the knee and for practical purposes had a slit up the back which when the rider was dismounted could be done up with a concealed flap and buttons. Cavalrymen's coats had a cape attached which was lined with yellow and could be buttoned up as an added protection against the cold.

A typical cavalry private poses to have his image made. Note the high collar of his shell jacket and the sword knot just visible dangling down from his sword. In combat, this would be wound around his wrist to stop him dropping his sabre. David Scheinmann.

In foul weather cavalrymen also wore a waterproof cape called a talma which had sleeves and reached to the knees.

While many cavalrymen were proud of their yellow trimmed shell jackets, some preferred single breasted plainer jackets without trim that were made to their

Sporting a revolver tucked into his waistbelt, and trousers tucked into his boots, this cavalryman wears an unusual dark blue overcoat. The regulation overcoat colour was sky blue, but in the haste to get men adequately uniformed, dark blue overcoats were also sometimes issued. David Scheinmann.

This smartly dressed and well equipped private wears his full dress Hardee hat converted into a much more manageable form of headgear. Also note the pistol holster on his belt and his bow tie. David Scheinmann.

own specifications. One Wisconsin cavalryman complained that his regulation jacket was 'oh so yellow that it made me sick.' Some states manufactured cavalry shell jackets which were close approximations of the official issue varying in the design of the piping, number of buttons and height of the collar.

The uniform of the 15th Pennsylvania Cavalry featured jackets slightly longer than issue shell jackets and they had red piping on the collar, sleeves and front. The piping was also formed into two rectangular shapes on either side of the jacket front. The shell jackets of the 2nd Missouri Volunteer Cavalry though trimmed in regulation yellow featured a curious diamond design on the jacket fronts, unique in the Union cavalry. 'All additions to or alterations of this uniform as prescribed are positively prohibited,' ordered the regiment's commander, Captain Lewis Merrill.

The men of Wilder's Mounted Brigade, Indiana and Illinois infantrymen who were 'galvanised' into cavalrymen to help fight Confederate cavalry and bushwackers harrassing supply lines, took no pride at all in the regulation yellow trimmed shell jackets they were issued with. 'We drew cavalry uniforms but cut off the yellow stripes from the seam of the pants and jackets, so that we might not be taken for cavalry,' wrote B.F. McGee, regimental historian of the 72nd Indiana Volunteer Infantry, an outfit not at all enamoured of their new uniforms.

The regular troopers of the 2nd Cavalry who before the war had been the 2nd Dragoons did not want to give up their orange facings at any price. 'Alas for the cherished orange it must give place to the gaudy yellow,' recalled by Theo F. Rodenborough in his book *From Everglade to Canyon with the Second Dragoons* (New York 1875). But orders permitted the former dragoons to wear their shell jackets with orange facings until they wore out and some men continued to wear them until well into the war.

Cavalry Headwear and Footwear

Like the infantry, cavalrymen were issued with a full dress Hardee hat, but the cavalry found it equally as uncomfortable, especially with the added stress of wearing the unwieldy hats while riding a horse. Like the infantry, cavalrymen would sometimes manipulate their hats into more comfortable shapes, but for the most part cavalrymen wore forage caps. Shoes were regulation bootees, but many cavalrymen were issued with or privately purchased knee length leather boots. Even more individualistic than the infantry, many cavalrymen were notorious for wearing civilian dress especially in the later stages of the war. In 1864, orders were issued to the men of the 2nd Iowa cavalry that they had to destroy all their civilian clothes and get back into regulation attire.

Amazingly some men even had to be ordered not to wear Confederate clothing. Some cavalrymen found that Confederate uniforms made out of jean cloth were cooler to wear than the standard issue Federal woollen uniforms.

Cavalry Equipment

Basic cavalry equipment was the sword belt with two slings on the left side from which the cavalryman's sabre was suspended and a pistol holster and cap

Shots showing cavalrymen mounted for campaign are comparatively rare but here we see what a cavalryman would have looked like in the field. Note the blanket tied up behind his saddle, the manageable way the cavalryman's sabre is hooked to his belt and the yellow stripe denoting his branch of service, running down his trouser seam. David Scheinmann.

pouch worn on the left side. Up until the mid-1850s the sabre had been suspended on a shoulder strap fitted with two sabre slings to support the weight of the heavy dragoon sabre. But when the light cavalry sabre was introduced and support pads were added to the back of cavalry jackets, there was no need for the shoulder strap which had proved to be unpopular. In August 1859 James Ewell Brown Stuart, then a lieutenant in the 1st cavalry before he found fame as a Confederate cavalry commander, had invented a brass device for attaching the sabre to the waistbelt and took a patent out on his invention, but only a few of the attachments ever saw service.

Ammunition for the cavalryman's pistol was kept in a pouch behind his holster. Belt holsters were a comparatively new innovation, single shot pistols had been carried in saddle holsters, but in 1851 the Colt firearms company began manufacturing leather belts with holsters and in 1855 the War Department began

This well appointed cavalry private, carries a distinctive looking sword with a particularly long pommel. It doesn't seem to be regulation and might be a personal purchase. David Scheinmann.

A Cavalry sergeant and private pose for the camera and show the disparity of dress you could expect to see in any cavalry regiment. The figure on the left wears a slouch hat while the figure on the right favours a forage cap. These two men look as if they are brothers or cousins. David Scheinmann.

ordering them for the cavalry. The most common way to wear a holster on the belt was on the right side with the butt of the holster pointing to the front.

The cavalryman's carbine was suspended from a sling worn over the left shoulder. Carbine slings were made out of black leather and were 56 inches long by $2\frac{1}{2}$ inches wide. Slings were adjusted with a brass buckle and a hook on the sling snapped into a ring on the carbine buckle. Cavalrymen wore their carbine slings mounted or dismounted. Carbine ammunition was usually carried in a box on the carbine belt. Cavalrymen either slung their canteens over their shoulders or looped them around the saddle. Haversacks were carried the same way and contained the same items as an infantryman's haversack. Other equipment carried by cavalrymen would include saddle bags, a length of rope and the horse's feed bag. Strapped over the pommel at the front of the saddle the horse soldier carried his rolled overcoat or talma. On the cantle behind the rider was a rolled blanket and tarpaulin.

Cavalry Horses

Early on, cavalrymen learned that their horses were their most valuable items of equipment. The credo of most cavalrymen was that they took care of their horses before they took care of themselves and while

The collar of this cavalry private's jacket looks uncomfortably high. He poses wearing a wide shoulder belt with a large brass buckle; and on this shoulder belt he would carry his carbine, suspended from a clip. David Scheinmann.

The distinctive yellow facings of this cavalryman's uniform mark him out to be a bugler. Note also the double seams of yellow on his trousers and the fancy stitching on the top of his boots. The bottom of his pistol holster can also be seen poking out from underneath his elbow. David Scheinmann.

an infantryman might be able to relax at the end of a day, cavalrymen spend hours grooming, feeding and watering their mounts.

In the winter of 1861 the 1st Maine Cavalry built stables for their horses while the men themselves slept out in the snow. But all the attention lavished on horses couldn't alter the effects of battle and supplying enough mounts was a problem until the Union War Department established the Cavalry Bureau in 1863. The bureau was given the responsibility of mounting and equipping all Union cavalrymen and in 1864 it supplied over 150,000 mounts to troopers.

Cavalry Saddles

The McClellan saddle became the Union cavalry's most widely used saddle during the Civil War and was still being issued to mounted troops in the American army as late as World War 2. The saddle was named after General George B. McClellan. McClellan saddles were extremely serviceable and were largely based on the saddles McClellan had seen being used

by Cossacks when he had been an observer in the Crimea. McClellan saddles were light and strong and easy on a horse's back.

They were also comfortable for the rider, apart from the early models covered in rawhide which often split. McClellan saddles were fitted with wooden stirrups with leather hoods. Under the saddle, a regulation blanket was folded like a pad. These blankets were usually dark blue wool with an orange border stripe and US in orange letters in the centre. Grey blankets with yellow trim were also issued.

Officers used McClellan saddles but favoured English saddles as well. Over the saddle, officers were supposed to drape a dark blue shabraque edged with gold lace.

Suitably saddled and equipped, all cavalry regiments should have been imposing sights, but the reality of a newly recruited cavalry regiment was often far from imposing, as remembered by Captain Vanderbilt in his History of the 10th New York

The straps attaching the officer's sword to his waistbelt are well shown in this picture. Civil War officers carried their swords hooked to the waistbelt with the hilts to the rear so that they hung parallel to the left leg. With his trousers tucked into his boots this man looks every inch a cavalry officer, but surprisingly he doesn't wear shoulder straps. David Scheinmann.

This cavalry officer wears his boots with the tops turned over and a curious flat brimmed hat. David Scheinmann.

Cavalry: 'Such a rattling, jerking, scrabbling cursing. I never heard before. Green horses some of them had never been ridden turned round and round, backed against each other, jumped up or stood up like trained circus horses. Some of the boys had never ridden anything since they galloped on a hobby horse and they clasped their legs close together, thus unconsciously sticking the spurs into their horses' sides.'

Sabres

Cavalrymen were usually either armed with the model 1840 heavy cavalry dragoon sabre or the 1856 light

Of all branches of the army, cavalry were renowned for their exotic dress, but many soldiers like this second lieutenant, remained soberly clothed. David Scheinmann.

cavalry sabre. The heavy cavalry sabre had a curved blade and a half basket guard, with a wooden grip covered with leather and wound with twisted brass wire. The light cavalry sabre which gradually replaced the 1840 pattern was similar except that the blade was lighter and shorter.

Although many cavalry actions in the war were fought by troopers shooting at each other from comfortable distances with revolvers, the shock of an attack by sabre swinging cavalry could still have important effects in the war. Both types of U.S. cavalry sabre were based on French patterns, and had sword knots attached to the guard which was worn around the wrist to stop the sabre being dropped in action. Like many infantrymen, some cavalrymen thought their appearance was not complete without at least one knife tucked into their belts as well as carrying a sabre. Most popular were hunting knives or the famous Bowie knife, the deadly looking broad bladed knife originated by Rezin Bowie the brother of the Alamo hero, Jim Bowie. Some of these Bowie knives even had large hilts and also made first class knuckle dusters.

Cavalry officer Colonel Max Friedman wears a regulation field grade officer's coat underneath his overcoat. David Scheinmann.

Pistols

The standard revolvers carried by Union cavalrymen were Colts. Other models included pistols manufactured by the Starr arms company and Remington, but the Colt revolver was the mainstay of the Union cavalry. The standard issue was the Colt 'Army' pistol which was .44 calibre, but the 0.36 calibre 'Navy' model was also popular because of its lighter weight.

Officer wearing regulation dress, but his boots are an odd
pointed shape and he also appears to be wearing Mexican
spurs with them. David Scheinmann.

Derided at the beginning of the war, Union cavalry turned into
an effective arm and this cavalryman has the air of a true
veteran. Unlike many cavalrymen he's retained his
cumbersome Hardee hat. David Scheinmann.

also widely used, but it was not as hard wearing and
was particularly susceptible to getting clogged with
black powder residue after the weapon was fired
several times.

The Smith carbine was unique in that it used
rubber cartridges which sealed the gap in the carbine
breech, but the drawback was that these unusual
cartridges could be difficult to remove. Other weapons
included Gibbs carbines, but these had to be broken
apart at the breech to insert a linen cartridge and the
weapon was later officially condemned as being
unserviceable.

Merrill carbines had a top loading mechanism but

Carbines

Carbines saw limited use with the infantry but they
were the standard arm of the cavalryman. A muzzle
loading rifle used on horseback is cumbersome and
impractical, the best way to arm a cavalryman was with
a breech loading carbine. The Sharps carbine was very
popular and the similarly designed Starr carbine was

Opposite.
Colonel Richard H. Rush, the founder of the famed Lancer
regiment that came to bear his name, wears a version of the
stiff high crowned patented whipple hat. It was one of the
more unusual items of headgear worn in the Civil War and
incorporated a rear flap to protect the wearer's neck.
U.S. Army Military History Institute / Jim Enos.

These men of Company I Rush's lancers were photographed on the Virginia Peninsula in 1862. The company guidon visible in this picture still survives and is in the collection of the War Library and Museum, Loyal Legion of the United States, Philadelphia. USAMMHI/Jim Enos.

they were not popular and neither were Burnside carbines, where cartridges again had a habit of jamming. The Spencer was the most serviceable weapon. The army bought 95,000 of them and they became the most popular cavalry carbine. Henry rifles, usually privately purchased, were also used but as they were longer than carbines they were often unwieldy on horseback and lacked a ring attachment to fit on to the cavalryman's shoulder belt.

Union Cavalry Officers' Dress

Regulation dress for officers comprised a dark blue frock coat single breasted for captains and lieutenants and double breasted for all other officers. Trousers were sky blue with a one eighth yellow welt on the seam, except for general officers whose trousers were left plain. Many officers didn't wear the frock coat in favour of shell jackets and many modified the standard uniform or even designed their own. An officer of the 1st Rhode Island Cavalry added gold tape to the the

collar and sleeves of his regulation frock coat, while Colonel Alfred Duffie of the same regiment created his own uniform which had a double breasted shell jacket, an embroidered chasseur cap and baggy chasseur trousers.

Colonel Israel Garrard of the 7th Ohio Cavalry also wore Chasseur trousers and his shell jacket was laden with gold loops. Alfred Torbert who began his Civil War career as colonel of the 1st New Jersey Infantry later became a cavalry commander and in 1864 wore a blue jacket with a wide collar and two rows of buttons. His black felt hat was creased down the centre with a single star in a wreath on the front. Crossed sabres were pinned on the right side. Sartorial style in cavalry officers varied from the elegant to the bizarre. It was not unusual to find officers wearing straw hats and battered Hardee hats with the brims coming down over their eyes. One officer of the 4th Pennsylvania Cavalry wore a coat even longer than a regulation frock coat, which he left unbuttoned to

Opposite.

Looking like a regular in the German army, this picture is of an unidentified United States Hussar taken in about 1860. Note the ornate trappings and Death's head motif on the busby. Michael J. McAfee.

Officers of the 27th New York Light Artillery wear special fatigue jackets with Russian shoulder knots, as prescribed in 1860 regulations. David Scheinmann.

show off his fancy striped shirt and white collar.

Lancers and Hussars

Lancers and Hussars had been a military tradition in Europe for many years and their influence eventually filtered through to America. The Union army never fielded large numbers of lancers or hussars, but a number of specialist units were recruited and saw good service. It is a little surprising that in the romantic notions of soldiering that persisted throughout the Civil War more of these type of units were not raised.

Two troops of regular cavalry were armed with lances as an experiment in the 1840s, but the idea didn't catch on. During the Mexican War, some members of the Mexican Spy Company, irregulars who provided scouts and guides for the American army carried lances, and a few lancer militia units flourished before the Civil War, but although the Union bought over 4,000 lances from contractors at the start of the Civil War, most of them ended up surplus to requirements, only a handful of lancer regiments was raised and few saw active service. One unit, the 1st Michigan Cavalry, who grandly called themselves the 1st United States Lancers, appear to have modelled themselves on the British 16th Lancers who had scattered the enemy with a charge at the Battle of Aliwal during Britain's Indian campaigns in the 1840s.

The Michigan Lancers wore a light coloured shell jacket and trousers and also sported jaunty pillbox forage caps, similar to the pillbox caps of the undress headwear of lancers in the British army. The men were fully equipped with lances as well as standard issue pistols, carbines and equipment; but they were later disbanded and never saw service. It was thought that the many Canadians in the ranks could cause trouble, particularly if their mother country Britain, became embroiled in the Civil War, taking sides with the South against the Union. The thought of Britain recognising the Confederacy and moving her troops stationed in Canada across the border to invade the North, was always a Union fear.

Opposite.

A member of the 1st U.S. Hussars poses for the camera in the unit's distinctive uniform which attracted many recruits, even in the weary days of the latter stages of the war. USAMHI/Jim Enos.

This artilleryman wears shoulder scales on his shell jacket. The sword which looks like a foot NCO's weapon, is probably a studio prop. David Scheinmann.

The most famous Union Lancer regiment was Rush's Lancers, the 6th Pennsylvania Cavalry. Very much an elite regiment it was raised in Philadelphia by Colonel H. Rush between August and October 1861, with financial aide from prominent citizens in the city. Rush's Lancers, who at first were just armed with sabres and colt revolvers, adopted the lance at the suggestion of General McClellan who had seen lancers in action during his time as a war observer in the Crimea. Rush's Lancers wore the regulation cavalry uniform with a few minor variations. The jacket collar had only one loop of braid and one button, instead of the regulation two. Made out of Norwegian fir, their lances were nine feet long and tipped with a blade 11 inches long.

A soldier wounded by such a blade could face a particularly unpleasant time. The lance points produced a narrow slit wound in the skin, which would heal on the surface, but debris carried in on the blade would fester underneath. A scarlet swallow-tailed pennon decorated each line and a leather sling was also attached to each lance so that lancers could carry them comfortably over their right shoulders. Each company of Rush's Lancers was also armed with 12 Sharps carbines for picket and scout duty.

As recorded in a sketch drawn by Winslow Homer of the regiment embarking at Alexandria Virginia for Old Point Comfort, the men were still wearing brass shoulder scales on their shell jackets in 1862. The men wore three variations of boots, the first were of soft leather which reached above the knee, the second were stiff leather boots with a protector for the knees in front and the third were a lower version of these boots reaching just up to the knees.

Some of Rush's lancers also seem to have done without boots, preferring shoes instead. Trousers worn this way would have been held down by straps under the instep. For full dress, Rush's lancers wore a high crowned hat with a flap that could be folded down over the neck like a havelock. Officers had black ostrich feathers attached to the sides of their hats and crossed sabres insignia on the front. Troopers wore their company letter in brass above stamped brass crossed sabres insignia. Enlisted men's fatigue caps had horizontal leather visors, sometimes with the brass letters RL regimental number 6 and crossed sabres on the top of the crowns.

Some historians have dismissed Lances used in the Civil War as novelty weapons that had little effect in combat, but Rush's Lancers saw some good service with theirs. Rush's Lancers first saw action shortly before the Battle of Hanover Courthouse in May 1862, when they charged an advance body of enemy cavalry and drove them away at lance-point. At Gaines' Mill, later in 1862, Rush's lancers were one of the units attacking an Alabama brigade and before South Mountain Rush's Lancers scattered a body of dismounted enemy cavalry in a wood. But one of their finest moments came at Antietam in September 1862 when a well timed charge scattered enemy artillery.

It seems that the psychological effect of a charging line of cavalrymen armed with lances had a tremendous effect on the enemy, but Union authorities deemed that lances were no longer suitable for mid 19th Century combat. In the summer of 1863 Rush's lancers reluctantly put their lances into storage and would never use them again. From then on, they fought like ordinary cavalrymen.

Opposite.

Dashing Colonel George E. Waring of the Fremont Hussars, wears an unusual style kepi and double breasted jacket under his cape. His unit was also known as the 1st Regiment Western Cavalry. Massachuseets Commandery Military Order of the Loyal Legion & the U.S. Army Military History Institute / Jim Enos.

To find a light artilleryman wearing a frock coat like this private is not unusual. The average artillery crew would have men wearing a wide variety of dress. David Scheinmann.

Hussars

After the battle of Gettysburg, the Union began to get increasingly war weary. In October 1863, President Lincoln issued a call for new regiments and the New Jersey authorities hit upon a brilliant idea to speedily attract recruits into one of the State's new cavalry regiments. The 3rd New Jersey Cavalry was called the 1st United States Hussars and recruits were promised a special hussar uniform, unlike any others worn in the Union army. Originally recruited by European armies, the attitude of devil-may-care hussar units with their colourful uniforms had won them an even greater reputation than lancers and recruits anxious to be dashing hussars were not slow to fill the ranks of the 3rd New Jersey Cavalry.

The uniform of the 1st United States Hussars was based on those worn by Austrian Hussars and the 3rd New Jersey quickly became known as the Butterflies because of their exotic dress. Their jackets were cut in the regulation Union cavalry style and trimmed in yellow but they were fastened with 12 large buttons

and two rows of 12 buttons formed a plastron at the side. Buttons were connected by double rows of yellow cord and cuffs were ornamented with yellow cord knots. Collars were edged with yellow tape and on each side featured an orange patch on which were set two yellow cords.

Hussars were issued with talmas which were made out of sky blue material with yellow braid and tassel, and often worn flung back over the shoulders. Trousers appear to have been standard issue, but had broad yellow stripes on the seams. One of the most distinctive parts of the uniform were the pill box hats worn by the men, which were worn cocked at an angle or like an ordinary forage cap. The hussars' caps had a chin strap and were trimmed yellow. Crossed sabre insignia and the company letter was worn on top of the cap and hussars wore a brass '3' in a wreath on the fronts of their caps. Officers' uniforms were even more spectacular with gold rather than yellow cord.

Cavalry veterans sneered at the Hussars who were at first confined to courier duties. But in the Shenandoah Valley in the latter stages of the war the regiment developed plenty of fighting skills including capturing an entire enemy regiment. They may have been called butterfles but the 1st United States Hussars also had a wasp-like sting.

Michigan Cavalrymen

The most famous Cavalry brigade of the American Civil War was Brigadier General George Armstrong Custer's Michigan Cavalry Brigade. Most enlisted men wore exact copies of the regulation cavalry shell jacket with its yellow braid, but one photograph of an enlisted man in Company G shows him wearing an unusual zouave style jacket. What really marked the Michigan Brigade out was its exceptional esprit de corps reflected in the uniform accessories it was issued with by its commander Brigadier General George Armstrong Custer.

Although best remembered for his defeat at the Little Big Horn 11 years after the war, Custer had an exemplary Civil War career which catapulted him from serving on the staff of Major General George B McClellan to command of the Michigan Cavalry Brigade and then command of the Army of the Potomac's third cavalry division. Custer took command of the Michigan cavalry Brigade in the

Opposite.
Lieutenant William Starks, adjutant of the 1st U.S. Hussars, wore this elaborate blue hip length pelisse edged in black astrakhan. His dark blue trousers look as if they have a single gold stripe running down the seams. USAMHI/Jim Enos.

Lieutenant Adam J. Slemmer of Company G. 1st United States Artillery, wears a frock coat and has a scholarly air of authority that typified many artillery officers during the American Civil War. David Scheinmann.

his men, by their long red neckties' wrote a captain.

In the way they kept their uniforms and polished their equipment, Custer's men were a cut above most standard cavalry regiments. Custer selected the most smartly dressed companies of the brigade to act as his escort and smartly dressed individual troopers were chosen to act as orderlies at Brigade headquarters.

Custer also instituted his own 'awards system' for officers of his brigade who had performed particularly well. At his own expense, he commissioned Custer Badges from the New York jewellers Tiffany and Co, which were proudly worn on the chest by recipients. Each Custer badge was a solid gold maltese cross surmounted by a single Brigadier's star. Custer's name was also inscribed on the cross and the award could only be given on his direct orders. One Custer badge recipient was Colonel James H. Kidd who was wounded at Falling Waters and Winchester. Kidd eventually succeeded Custer as commander of the Michigan Cavalry Brigade.

Union Artillery

Many distinguished Civil War commanders served their military apprenticeships with the artillery during the Mexican War, a conflict which became a golden age for this branch of the service. One company from each of the four American artillery regiments was designated as a light battery and with each member of the battery mounted could manoeuvre as fast as the cavalry. One commander, Sam Ringgold, even had special uniforms issued to his command that included dark blue jackets, faced red, sky blue trousers, and a shako with red cords that became known as the Ringgold cap.

After the Mexican War, the artillery started going into decline. For the sake of economy many of the light batteries were dismounted and at the start of the Civil War there were only five regular artillery regiments. Each regiment had 12 companies, but only two of these companies in each regiment were equipped as field artillery with guns and horses. The rest of the companies served as infantry or heavy artillery manning the cumbersome heavy guns on the coast.

Artillery Uniforms

Broadly speaking, there were two types of uniforms worn by the Union artillery. Heavy artillery who manned costal defences or the fortifications around Washington wore the infantry regulation dress of frock coats and Hardee hats. Light artillery who served in the field officially wore shell jackets like the cavalry but artillery jackets were trimmed with scarlet

summer of 1863 just days before the Battle of Gettysburg when Custer led the Wolverines, as his brigade become known in a decisive action against Confederate cavalry. In admiration of their leader some of Custer's men began to sport red neckties like the one he wore and before long it became fashionable in the entire brigade. 'You could always tell Custer and

braid, marking the artillery's branch of service. Unique to the light artillery was the dragoon style Ringgold cap with its high peak and red horsehair plumes.

In 1858, light artillerymen were ordered to wear Hardee hats like the rest of the army, but they were unwilling to part with their Ringgold caps and in early 1859 they were authorised to wear scarlet cap cords and tassels on the hats and to place crossed cannon and regimental numerals on the fronts. In practice it seems that the elaborate headgear saw little field service being replaced by kepis or forage caps.

In practice a field battery would wear a variety of uniform styles and infantry sack coats were common. In 1860 the government authorised a special jacket for light artillery officers, which had Russian shoulder knots of gilt cord, but many officers also wore the regulation nine button frock coat in the field, or like infantry and cavalry officers adapted dress to suit their fancy.

Northern artillery units never quite boasted the same individuality in their uniforms as some artillery units in Confederate service like the Washington Artillery of New Orleans or the Richmond Howitzers, but they performed admirably. At Gettysburg, the 9th Massachusetts Artillery who had previously seen precious little action manning the defences of Washington found themselves in the thick of the action when almost single handedly they delayed the charge of a Confederate brigade and bought precious time for Union troops to entrench on Cemetery Ridge.

Manpower shortages late in the war meant that many Union heavy artillery regiments who had little service posted in the defences around Washington, were ordered to go to the front. Their smart frock coats and Hardee hats set them apart from the other soldiers and they became objects of derision, but the 'bandbox soldiers' proved they could fight. In May 1864 the 1st Maine Heavy Artillery lost 476 men at the battle of Harris farm and would also sustain heavy casualties at Petersburg.

Cannon
The muzzleloading field piece was the standard workhorse of the artillery of the Civil War and usually six guns were grouped into a battery. The field artillery piece that saw the most use in the Civil War was the 12 pounder Napoleon 1857 model. A smooth bore weapon, it was ideal at close ranges against enemy infantry. Parrott guns had breeches reinforced by a thick metal jacket and were accurate up to a range of two miles. Other deadly weapons in the North's artillery arsenal included three inch ordnance rifles which were cast in wrought iron. Columbiad guns, manned by the heavy artillery on the coast, saw little service.

Generals, Staff, and Special Units

Union Generals were authorised to wear double breasted frock coats with dark blue velvet collars and cuffs. Major-generals had nine buttons placed in threes in two rows and brigadier generals had eight buttons in each row placed in pairs. Generals wore white shirts under their coats, black ties and usually a dark blue waistcoat with nine buttons. Dark blue trousers completed a typical general's clothing. The truly extravagant part of a Union general's uniform was the French style *chapeau de bras* he was authorised to wear. The *chapeau de bras* had been cancelled in the dress regulations of 1851 but was re-authorised in the regulations of 1859. In practise though most generals preferred to wear smart black felt Hardee hats pinned

up on the right side with an embroidered gold eagle badge and with three black ostrich feathers on the left. Around their waists, generals wore a silk sash over a sword belt. The sashes were tied over the left hip.

Generals' overcoats were dark blue with four silk buttons at the front and a cape, a double silk knot on each sleeve indicated rank. Away from official work many generals preferred to wear officers' sack coats in the field, but some Union army generals were lacking in sartorial style. Surrendering at Appomattox Court House in 1865 General Lee wore a bright new uniform and a jewelled dress sword, but General Grant who had finally been able to wear Lee's army down, turned up to the surrender ceremony dressed very shabbily. 'Grant covered with mud in an old faded uniform looked like a fly on a shoulder of beef,' recalled one of Grant's staff, Colonel Amos Webster.

Staff officers wore basically the same basic uniforms but their cuffs and collars were dark blue. Field grade officers had two rows of seven buttons down the fronts of their frock coats, while company grade officers had a row of nine buttons. Epaulettes carried their corps and rank insignia, and rank insignia was also worn on dark blue shoulder straps. Colonels had a silver eagle, lieutenant colonels had two silver oak leaves, captains had two gold bars at each end of their shoulder straps while second lieutenants had a single gold bar at each end. First lieutenants' shoulder straps were plain. Staff officers' trousers had gold braid cord down the seams, their hats were decorated with black and gold cords and their

Major General Nathananiel Prentiss Banks in full dress, including an ornate chapeau. David Scheinmann.

Opposite.
This portrait of Brigadier General Dan Sickles details the velvet standing collar of his frock coat and the single silver star that designates his rank can be seen on his epaulette. David Scheinmann.

Brigadier General Israel B. Richardson was killed at the battle of Antietam in 1862, one of the 47 generals on both sides who died in the war. David Scheinmann.

waist sashes were crimson.

U.S. Marines

The US Marine Corps in the American Civil War didn't have the same prominence in the Army that the Marines occupy today. The corps numbered under 5,000 men and despite the bad performance of a detachment of Marines at First Bull Run, who

Brigadier General George Brinton McClellan and his wife. The two separate rows of eight buttons designating his rank can clearly be seen on McClellan's regulation frock coat. David Scheinmann.

together with the Fire Zouaves of the 11th New York broke and ran during a heavy artillery bombardment, the Marines performed well in many coastal operations. For full dress, Marines wore dark blue frock coats with yellow braid and scarlet trim. For campaign dress, they wore single breasted frock coats trimmed in red on the collars and white linen trousers which were very suited to the humid conditions on the coast which they often fought in. Officers commonly wore double breasted frock coats with Russian knots to indicate rank. Caps were Chasseur pattern kepis with a brass infantry horn and M on the front. Marines also had white buff equipment belts with brass rectangular belt plates and NCOs wore their yellow silk chevrons the tips up, not down like the army. *(continued on p. 92)*

Opposite.

Major General Ambrose Burnside wears a nine buttoned frock coat. His style of beard was much imitated and called a Burnside. David Scheinmann.

Union Cavalry, Five Forks, April 1865.

Of all Union commanders, none had such a reputation or theatrical taste in uniforms as George Armstrong Custer. Loved by his men but sometimes resented by fellow officers, Custer had a meteoric rise to fame during the Civil War and wore flamboyant clothes to match.

Photographs of Custer taken early in the war when he was a captain. show him to be quite tamely dressed in a short dark blue jacket open at the collar to reveal a flowing neckerchief, and sky blue trousers. But when Custer was promoted to Brigadier General at the age of 23, he wore a black velvet uniform adorned with gold lace. One contemporary report said that he looked like 'a circus rider gone mad'. Rather like his hero, the Napoleonic Cavalry general Murat, Custer had a taste for exotic uniforms and the panache to carry them off.

One of Custer's best known uniforms is the one he's wearing in this painting. Custer adopted this style of uniform when he was promoted to major general in the autumn of 1864. His broad brimmed hat, and his sailor's shirt with white stars and white trim on the collar remained from his old uniform, but with them Custer now wore a cut down regulation double breasted officer's frock coat and blue trousers with gold stripes. Finishing off the ensemble was Custer's trademark, his red necktie.

Some may have laughed at Custer's uniforms but standing out on the battlefield Custer was an inspiration to many men in the Union cavalry. James H. Kidd who succeeded Custer to the command of the Michigan Cavalry Brigade, wrote: 'That garb, fantastic as at first sight it appeared to be, was to be the distinguishing mark which showed us where in the thick of battle we were to seek our leader.'

The two troopers behind Custer wear regulation shell jackets with the distinctive yellow trim on the collar, fronts and cuffs. Custer and his men are all wielding sabres and doubtless bore them in many other battles and skirmishes, but how how much use sabres saw in Civil War combat and how effective they were, has been the subject of much debate. Assessing the relative values of the Union Cavalry's use of swords or sabres in Civil War battles is difficult, because of conflicting reports written at the time. One account records Custer plunging his sabre into a Confederate cavalryman. Major Leonidas Scranton of the 2nd Michigan Cavalry wrote: 'Pistols are useless. I have known regiments that have been in the field over two years that have never used their pistols in action. At a charge, the sabre is the weapon.' Painting by Chris Collingwood.

This first sergeant of Light Artillery is pictured wearing a regulation shell jacket and the red stripe down his trouser seam designates his branch of service. David Scheinmann.

Major General Gordon Meade was a no nonsense commander and made an imposing figure in his uniform. Two stars are visible on his shoulder straps. David Scheinmann.

Inventor turned Union officer, Hiram Berdan founded the crack Berdan's sharpshooters. The uniforms of Berdan's Sharpshooters officers were similar to the men's, but made out of better quality cloth. David Scheinmann.

Marines carried unusual knapsacks which had two carrying straps, an adjustable breast strap and was marked 'USM' on the back. Marines were originally armed with 1855 rifle muskets and officers carried infantry officers' sabres. Additional arms for Marine officers would include revolvers of the same type carried by infantry officers.

Berdan's Sharpshooters

The green forage caps and uniforms of Hiram Berdan's two regiments of sharpshooters made them unique in the Union forces during the American Civil War. They were elite regiments and the selection process to join as described by Lieutenant Colonel William M. Ripley in his book *Vermont Riflemen in the War for the Union*, was a tough one: 'it was required that a recruit should possess a good moral character, a sound physical development and in other respects come within the usual requirements of the army regulations. It was required of them that before enlistment they should justify their claim to be called "sharp shooters" by such a public exhibition of their skill as should fairly entitle them to the name and warrant a reasonable expectation of usefulness in the

Opposite.
This Berdan's Sharpshooters enlisted man wears the unit's distinctive frock coat and characteristically his trousers are tucked into tan coloured gaiters. Michael J. McAfee.

Two engineer privates pose with the distinctive turreted insignia of the unit clearly visible on their forage caps. David Scheinmann.

One of the better photographs of Major General Ulysses S. Grant who cared little for smart dress, but who habitually wore a bow tie. David Scheinmann.

field. The recruit should in effect be able to place ten bullets in succession within a ten-inch ring at a distance of two hundred yards.'

Colonel Berdan was virtually given a free hand in the choice of the sharpshooters' uniforms, but strangely enough his first choice for the sharpshooters' clothing was not green, but blue. Originally, Berdan wanted his men to wear loose fitting heavy dark blue sack coats with metal buttons. The sack coats would have a black fringe around the collar and bottom. The men would wear soft felt hats ornamented with black feathers. Possibly influenced by the green uniforms of the German Jaeger units who had served with the British during the American Revolution, Berdan later changed his mind thinking that blue would be too conspicuous in the field, writing that 'The green-ness would better correspond in the leafy season with the colors of the foliage'.

The men wore forest green double breasted frockcoats piped light green and their trousers were described as being of an Austrian blue-grey colour. By 1862, these were exchanged for dark green trousers,

although some of the men still wore the lighter coloured pants. Berdan's Sharpshooters historian Captain C. A. Stevens wrote that the men's clothing presented a striking contrast to the regulation blue of the infantry and a correspondent for the *New York Post* picturesquely said that the green clad sharpshooters reminded him of Robin Hood's outlaws.

The original overcoats issued to Berdan's Sharpshooters were made of grey felt and many if not all were trimmed light green like the men's frock coats. It was a poorly conceived garment not only because in wet weather the material went very stiff, but because the men could be confused with the enemy. Lieutenant Colonel Ripley of the Sharpshooters wrote: 'Certain grey overcoats and soft hats of the same rebellious hue were promptly exchanged for others of a color in which they were less apt to be shot by mistake by their own friends. The

Opposite.

Doctor Alexander Mott of the medical department wears the shoulder straps of a lieutenant or major. David Scheinmann.

Hospital steward wearing the distinctive green armband of medical orderlies. David Scheinmann.

This sergeant of the Veteran Reserve Corps wears the unit's light blue uniform. David Scheinmann.

fighting taught them the lesson that the gray overcoats and soft hats had to go, lest they be shot by their own friends.'

Some period photos of Berdan's Sharpshooters show individual men wearing sack coats rather than frock coats. These might be ordinary issue infantry sack coats issued because of clothing shortages or they may be special sackcoats of green material like the Sharpshooters' standard issue frock coats. It's almost

impossible to tell, from old black and white photographs. Berdan's Sharpshooters' forage caps were made out of heavy wool and were forest green in colour. Visors differed from the standard enlisted man's cap and resemble the pattern of a McDowell forage cap visor. The men originally sported ostrich plumes in their kepis, but it seems that with rigorous combat in the field these would have quickly worn out.

Apart from their green forage caps, the 1st regiment of Berdan's Sharpshooters and possibly the 2nd regiment, were also issued with another type of headgear. It was described as 'a gray round hat with a leather visor, a flap to cover the neck and holes for ventilation.' These unwieldy hats were discarded in the spring of 1862, not least because men wearing them could again be mistaken for Confederates.

Berdan's Sharpshooters often wore a distinctive brass badge on their forage caps, which had the initial U.S.S.S. surrounded by a wreath. Soldiers joked that the letters stood for Unfortunate Soldiers Sadly Sold and not United States Sharpshooters. Another unique feature of the Sharpshooters' uniforms were the black non-reflective hard rubber buttons on their uniforms. No other unit in the Union army is reported to have worn them. Knapsacks carried by the sharpshooters were of a Prussian design and were made of tanned leather with the hair on the outside. They were heavier than regulation knapsacks but apparently fitted the men's backs well and were very roomy inside. It appears that Berdan's Sharpshooters were a particular fine looking unit, who revelled in the distinctiveness of their uniforms. 'By our dress we were known far and wide and the appellation of "green coats" was soon acquired,' wrote Captain C.A. Stevens, the regimental historian.

Engineers

Building roads and bridges the Corps of Engineers had an unglamorous but neccessary job. Sometimes they were also called to fight. The regular Union army's small engineer corps was bolstered by volunteer engineer regiments including the 50th New York Engineers and the 1st Michigan. Engineers wore infantry frock coats trimmed in yellow, with nine buttons down the front and two on each cuff. A distinctive badge worn by engineers on their forage was a brass turretted castle. Strangely the men of Elmer Ellsworth's United States Zouave cadets also wore this insignia on the collars of their Chasseur dress; possibly because Ellsworth planned to form an engineer battalion in the Cadets, or because he simply like the design.

Engineer officers wore standard dress, but their trousers featured a gold seam stripe down each leg. Topographical engineers who were responsible for making maps, wore special buttons on their coats marked 'TE' and even when they were merged into the Corps of Engineers they jealously guarded the privilege of wearing their unusual buttons.

In the field, engineers were issued with overalls to protect their uniforms from mud and a special pioneer

In the early days of the war, men of the 5th New York Volunteer Infantry used to wear havelocks under their fezzes and sometimes even tucked them up around their chins. Brian C. Pohanka.

corps made up of men drawn from other regiments was created in the Union Army of the Cumberland. On their left shoulders, the men wore a special cloth badge with a crossed hatchet motif.

The Signal Corps

The Signal Corps was another small but useful part of the Union Army. Strangely, they appear to have been dressed in cavalrymen's jackets and trousers and although not seeing active combat were well armed with revolvers.

Enlisted signalmen wore badges with crossed signal flags motifs on their sleeves. During the Peninsular Campaign when there was a brief craze for using manned balloons to look down on enemy positions, a special unit of signalmen was created who wore badges with 'BC', standing for Balloon Corps, motifs on their sleeves.

Veteran Reserve Corps and Medics

The Veteran Reserve Corps was created in 1863 as the

Soldiers battered their hats into a variety of shapes to personalise them. This cavalry or artillery private, favoured a stovepipe effect with his hat. David Scheinmann.

Invalid Reserve Corps, but this name proved unpopular so it was changed. The Corps was composed of invalid soldiers performing light work or garrison duties freeing able soldiers for the field. Some companies of the Reserve Corps actually saw some combat themselves at Fort Stevens in the Washington defences when they helped to repel a raid by Jubal Early's Confederate cavalry. During the skirmish, the Corps lost five men killed.

Men of the Invalid Corps wore sky blue cavalry style jackets, but with shoulder straps. The colour of these jackets was reminiscent of the jackets worn by soldiers in the Mexican War. Ordinary sack coats were worn for fatigue duties and trousers and forage caps were regulation. Officers of the Veteran Reserve Corps wore sky blue frock coats, with dark blue velvet collars, cuffs and shoulder straps. Their sky blue trousers had double stripes of dark blue cloth down the seams.

The first proper ambulance corps was established in the Army of the Potomac in 1862. Before that the only people taking immediate care of wounded

soldiers were bandsmen acting as stretcher bearers and about 10 soldiers relieved from normal duties by each regiment, but these men were usually misfits. In the Army of the Potomac each infantry regiment was eventually provided with three ambulances, each cavalry regiment had two ambulances and each artillery regiment had one. Privates in the Ambulance Corp were to wear two inch wide bands around their caps and a green half chevron two inches broad on each arm.

Army surgeons wore majors' uniforms and assistant surgeon's wore captains' uniforms. Their dark blue trousers had gold cord running down each leg seam and their sashes were usually emerald green. Though medical care was far from perfect soldiers could expect far better treatment if they were wounded than their forbears in previous wars. Assisting surgeons in the army was a team of medical cadets, dressed as second lieutenants and recruited from unqualified doctors in training.

Hospital stewards helped doctors and they wore a frock coat trimmed with crimson. On each sleeve they wore distinctive green sashes and their trousers had crimson stripes down the seams of each leg. For formal oocasions, stewards were authorised to wear brass shoulder scales on each shoulder.

Personalising Uniforms

During the Civil War, many regiments were renowned for the individual touches they made to their uniforms. The Bucktails who sported strips of deer hide in their kepis have already been mentioned, but they were far from being the only Union regiment who stood out even though they wore regulation army dress. Some members of the the 124th New York Volunteer Infantry, who were mainly recruited from Orange County New York State, wore orange ribbons looped in their buttonholes when they left to join up with the rest of the army and at the Battle of Chancellorsville in May 1863, where the regiment lost two fifths of its men the 124th's commander Augustus Van Horne Ellis urged his men forward using their nickname. The craze for men of the 124th pinning orange ribbons to their coats was noted by Private Henry Howard in his diary: 'One of the late (General Amiel) Whipple's aides came through the ward and saw the

Opposite.

The way Union soldiers wore their uniform differed greatly. Some looked immaculate while others, like this soldier wearing his sack coat open favoured a devil-may-care appoach. This soldier has an oilskin cover on his forage cap. David Scheinmann.

Alonzo Hamblin

red tape on one of the men's buttonholes. He said "there is an orange blossom" and put his hand in his pocket and gave him a dollar.'

Already a fine unit, the ribbons gave the 124th New York an even greater sense of identity and purpose as they showed at the Battle of Gettysburg in July 1863, two months after they had been nicknamed Orange Blossoms at Chancellorsville. During the Battle of Gettysburg the 124th was stationed near Devil's Den and lost many more men trying to force back a Confederate attack that ultimately overwhelmed them.

A frock coat worn by Major John H Thompson of the 124th New York still survives and has an orange ribbon still tied around the fifth buttonhole. The ribbon is nine inches long and five eighths of an inch wide.

Civil War soldiers wore a wide variety of unofficial insignia. Some menbers of Rush's Lancers wore badges with crossed lances and the men of the 11th New York Volunteer Infantry, the Fire Zouaves, were very fond of wearing the badges of the various hose, hook and ladder companies of the firefighting crews they had belonged to before the war.

Identity discs

Modern soldiers are issued with dog tags, but during the American Civil War there was no way of identifying soldiers killed in battle. Many soldiers before going into combat would pin slips of paper with their name and regiment to the backs of the coats in the hope that if they were killed they could be identified. Sometimes they also scratched their names into their waistbelts, or stenciled them on their haversacks, canteens or knapsacks. Many soldiers bought identity discs which were advertised by jewellers in popular magazines of the day like *Harper's Weekly*.

Identity discs usually came in two types. The first was a badge made out of gold or silver engraved with the soldier's name and unit. The second were made out of brass or lead and similar to modern dog tags were bored with a hole through which a length of

Bucktails were not the only soldiers to personalise their headgear. This infantry private wears an unusally shaped hat with a sprig of greenery or a feather stuck in it. David Scheinmann

string could be threaded for the disc to be worn around the wearer's neck. These tags usually had a patriotic motto on one side, with the owner's name and regiment on the other. Some soldiers even had their discs stamped with the names of the battles they had fought in. Civilian manufacturers sometimes set up shop on roadsides to supply passing troops with discs. In 1864 the entire 14th New Hampshire Infantry was supplied with discs stamped out by a dealer as the regiment marched through West Virginia, heading for the Shenandoah Valley.

Union State Uniforms

Although the Union Army had developed a regulation uniform, many States jealously guarded the right to equip their own volunteers. Most States had drawn up their own uniform regulations and many men joining units in these States started the war in uniforms that not only were locally prescribed, but in many cases were manufactured in the State concerned. Some of these States followed the U.S. Army regulations almost exactly, but before 1861 States didn't draw uniforms from army stocks. Regulations in other states varied the design and colour of local volunteer uniforms, but some volunteer units, like the many Zouave and Chasseur regiments already described, chose to ignore State regulations completely and designed their own fanciful uniforms; but thousands of volunteers went to war in regulation state Uniforms.

After 1851 there was a growing trend, notably in Northern cities, to provide volunteer regiments with a standardised uniform, particularly with regiments where each different company designed its own uniforms and could have a motley appearance on parade. Wealthy cities like New York seem to have been particularly successful in getting many of their volunteer regiments neatly uniformed in standard dress. In 1859, the 69th New York State Militia changed its green tail coats for blue uniforms in keeping with the 1858 New York militia regulations and was a typical volunteer regiment that began the war wearing State regulation dress. A report in October 1859 noted: 'The uniform of this regiment is all new and according to the regulation as adopted. The change in the uniform of this regiment is highly creditable to them as the one they have discarded was good and they could have retained it; but, desirous of conforming to the regulation colour, they sacrificed their prejudice for a color that was cherished by them

and adopted blue.'

The 69th received coats based on US army regulations which were described as: 'A single breasted frock coat of dark blue cloth with a skirt extending to within four inches of the bend of the knee. One row of nine buttons on the breast, placed at equal distances; stand-up collar to rise no higher than to permit the chin to turn freely over it, to hook in front of the bottom, and slope thence up and backward at an angle of thirty degrees on each side; cuffs pointed according to pattern, and to button with two small buttons at the outer seam. Collar and cuffs edged with a welt of scarlet cloth. Narrow lining for skirt of the coat of same material and colour of the coat; pockets in the

The three standing figures in this photograph are wearing short jackets with shoulder straps, typical of many New York units. David Scheinmann.

New York infantry privates in camp wearing state regulation jackets rounded at the front. David Scheinmann.

folds of skirts with one button at the hip to range with the lowest buttons on the breast; no buttons at the ends of the pockets.'

It appears that the regulation coats were often longer than specified, extending as far as the knee. The 69th added narrow red shoulder straps to their coats secured by a small button, and on top of these for full dress they wore scarlet worsted epaulettes.

New York regulation trousers on the eve of the American Civil War, were based on regulation Army trousers worn before 1854 and they were sky blue with a one eighth of an inch scarlet welt on the seams. Full dress caps were based on the army regulation cap of 1851 and were made out of dark blue cloth on a felt body, but varied a little in dimensions. The crowns were about six inches in diameter and were designed to tilt forwards slightly and had a black leather band around the bottom. The caps had visors and a black leather chinstrap attached to the helmet by two buttons.

Officers' dress conformed to the 1858 pattern New York regulations which was a close approximation of US standard army patterns, except that the skirts of

coats were longer. Regulations stated: 'All officers shall wear a frock coat of dark blue cloth, the waist to extend to the top of the hip and the skirt to within one inch of the bend of the knee.' The coats were lined black and the epaulettes and shoulder straps were of the standard New York and regular army pattern. Coats were worn with sky blue trousers which had scarlet welts down each side bordered with gold lace. New York regulation officers' caps were to be made out of dark blue cloth but the crowns were meant to lie flat without any stiffening inside.

Regulations adopted in April 1861, prescribed dark blue jackets for New York troops, which were meant to have eight buttons on the front and reach down four inches from a man's waistbelt. Trousers were described as being light blue with a full cut in the legs. New York state issued overcoats were to be of a similar pattern as the regular army.

The New York issue regulation forage caps were very unsual. They were supposed to incorporate a

Opposite.

This well armed volunteer wears a typical state issued jacket with shoulder straps. He's also wearing a state buckle, but it's almost impossible to make out the full design. David Scheinman.

water proof cover similar to a havelock, which fell to the shoulder. This complicated accessory was designed to be buttoned on the kepi visor and it was also fitted with strings so that it could be tied at the chin. Regulations also stated that each enlisted man should be provided with two cotton flannel shirts, two pairs of stout woollen socks, a pair of stout shoes and a waterproofed blanket.

The most usual jacket issued to New York Volunteers was dark blue with a low standing collar. These jackets had light blue trim, although some jackets have piping of a blue green colour. New York jackets had shoulder straps, similar to the straps found on many Confederate jackets, but the New York jacket shoulder straps were trimmed light blue. Eight large brass buttons with the state insignia were worn down the front of the jacket, featuring the coat of arms of the City of New York and the motto 'Excelsior'.

Jackets were lined with cotton and a narrow pocket, called a slash pocket, was often a feature over the left breast. Jacket sleeves had two small buttons on each cuff, but these were for decorative purposes only: the cuffs could not be opened. New York State jackets were issued to more than 100 regiments from New York and New York state and the majority were good, hard wearing garments.

In 1863 New York wanted to clothe all its many militia units the same way, with dark blue jackets which had pointed white cuffs. Two styles of uniform were available; the first was the ever popular Chasseur pattern with a long Chasseur jacket, a piped cap of dark blue and full sky blue trousers. The second comprised a dark blue polka jacket trimmed with white piping. This uniform had the same cap as the Chasseur uniform and sky blue trousers.

Trousers were a light indigo colour and had tape edging around the pockets for militiamen who wore Chasseur jackets. Dark blue kepis were provided with the state coat of arms worn on the front. Mounted units of the militia wore regular cavalry style jackets with forage caps or brimmed hats. Buttons again featured the state coat of arms and officers and non commissioned officers had handsome rectangular sword belts with an NY motif raised in silver. Enlisted men wore standard 'SNY' beltplates.

It generally looks as if New York's enlisted men armed and equipped by the State were well catered for. In 1862 the Quartermaster General of the State of New York issued the 143rd New York Volunteer Infantry, another typical regiment with this bonanza of items; 1,160 infantry jackets, 1,000 infantry trousers, 1,000 infantry great coats, 1,600 great coat straps, 1,000 caps, 1,016 letters, 3,043 numbers, 1,015

blankets, 2,000 shirts, 2,100 drawers, 2,100 pairs of socks and 1,000 pairs of shoes.

Connecticut's militia system dated back to the 17th century and boasted the longest established militia units in the Union. Indeed, two of its present National Guard regiments can claim direct descendancy from units formed in the State over 300 years ago. The State was proud of its volunteer forces but on the eve of the Civil War many units were lacking adequate uniforms. The *Military Gazette*, published in New York, claimed that Connecticut's eight State regiments were 'in a most sickly and ephemeral condition' and such comments prompted the Connecticut authorities to improve the quality and design of State issued uniforms. A state uniform had originally been adopted by Connecticut in 1847 which with minor exceptions was similar to the uniform worn by the U.S. Army.

In 1851 Connecticut based its State uniforms on the new pattern uniforms being introduced into the Regular Army, the Governor of Connecticut felt that these uniforms would combine 'the essential requisites of neatness, cheapness, comfort and utility'. The new uniforms cost less than 15 dollars and all militia units were ordered to wear them when their existing uniforms wore out.

The new uniform for officers and men was a dark blue frock coat and trousers. Buttons were arranged the same as the Regular Army. Dark blue cloth caps were part of the uniform which had distinctively coloured pompons. Officers' overcoats were double breasted, while those for enlisted men were single breasted. Strangely response was slow from the militia units to equip themselves with these state issued uniforms. The Adjutant General said that units not conforming to the new uniform pattern should be fined and even planned to circulate a series of coloured prints depicting the uniform so there could be no excuse in volunteers not knowing about them.

Eventually four fifths of the Connecticut militia were outfitted in State uniforms which because of their accessories were some of the most colourful of the American Civil War. Two companies of each Connecticut regiment were usually classed as rifle companies and wore green pompons on their caps, green piping on their coats and green trouser stripes.

An independent rifle regiment was raised in 1861

Opposite.

This private of the 65th New York Volunteers who were known as the 1st U.S. Chasseurs, is wearing a New York Chasseur jacket trimmed light blue. The 65th's forage caps were very unusual. They were standard issue forage caps with the peaks and chinstraps removed. David Scheinmann.

and all the men had green facings. But although their uniforms were smart, the armaments issued to some of the men, as recalled by one militiaman, were less than adequate. 'They brought out a lot of old Springfield smooth-bore muskets for us, the same as they had already given to some of the other companies of our regiment. We just informed them that we were not going to carry them guns - we preferred Sharps rifles. We were a rifle company; hadn't we got green stripes sewed on our pants?'

Connecticut artillerymen wore scarlet pompons and had scarlet piping and trouser stripes. Cavalrymen had orange facings and many wore felt hats and plumes instead of dress caps. Volunteers were usually uniformed and equipped by the towns from which they came. The blue cloth for the uniforms was cut up by teams of local ladies and made into uniforms. Until proper forage caps could be obtained many men took the stiffening out of their formal dress caps and wore them with the crowns flat.

In early 1861 supplies of blue cloth ran out so that one Connecticut volunteer infantry regiment had to be uniformed in grey. Their uniforms were based on the famous grey uniforms worn by the 7th Regiment New York State Militia, the Old Greybacks. The men were also issued with a light grey cap.

Connecticut regiments were renowned for the formality of their dress and they were especially noted for the time they took polishing their brasswork, but Connecticut regiments like regiments in general suffered from uniforms made of poor quality cloth, some of which didn't last beyond the first months of the war. Four Connecticut infantry regiments were issued with trousers and jackets made out of a cheap blend of wool and cotton that quickly fell apart during the rigours of the Bull Run campaign. It's said that when the men returned home many of them paraded in trousers made up out of old blankets and some even wore items of captured Confederate clothing.

Connecticut full dress shakos, some of which saw service during the War bore the state coat of arms; vines with grapes over the motto *Qui transtulit sustinet*. Officers bore wore the letters CM as their badge. Buttons on state issued uniforms also bore the same motto as the shakos. Despite the previous comments of the rifleman bemoaning the fact that his unit was not well equipped with weapons, it seems that Connecticut volunteers issued weapons by the State were generally better off than the volunteers from many other states.

Connecticut was a heavily industrialised state and was able to buy its weapons from a variety of local manufacturers, including the Colt Firearms Company.

Samuel Colt even planned to raise, arm and equip a regiment at his own expense. Colt wanted to raise a regiment composed of tall men of good character and insisted on the right of being able to select all the officers personally, but authorities deemed that the regiment would be elitist and Colt's request to raise a body of troops for the Union was eventually turned down.

Connecticut troops were issued with several unusual items of equipment by the state, including a unique canteen and ration box combined. Many of the issued knapsacks seem to have been particularly uncomfortable because the carrying straps meant the whole weight was concentrated on a man's lung area. The rubber knapsacks also had an appalling smell. The *New Haven Daily Register* wrote: 'They are the meanest specimens of equipment that you can smell about as far as they can be seen.'

The state of Maine issued many of its volunteer forces with uniforms which came in a bewildering variety of shades of grey. In 1861 troops received frock coats with eight buttons stamped with the Maine coat of arms down the front, grey trousers and grey forage caps. These could be in Canada grey or were issued in light grey, cadet grey and a bluish cadet grey colour. Blue uniforms were also issued to some regiments in the state which unlike the regulation Army uniforms had dark blue trousers, instead of light blue kerseys. Indeed for some reason Maine troops always preferred wearing dark blue to light blue trousers.

Soldiers from Maine had Mexican war style waistbelt plates marked with 'VMM' with stood for Volunteer Militia of Maine. These waistbelts were smaller than the regulation size, but the men's cartridge box plates also marked 'VMM' came in the same size as regulation army cartridge box plates. Maine soldiers were armed with 1855 rifle muskets and 1858 pattern Enfields from State stores.

It seems that Maine state issued uniforms, unlike some uniforms issued by other States, were not worn long into the war. The majority of men replaced the State dress with regulation army dress after they marched to Washington in the summer of 1861. Doubtless some Maine items did stay in service, including the State's waist belt plates and cartridge box plates.

A poor frontier state, Minnesota could not afford to outfit its troops in the smart uniforms many of the smart Eastern states supplied. The uniform issued to Minnesota troops reflected their background and comprised rugged thick shirts which in the main seem to have been red or checkered, black trousers, and wide brimmed black hats. Parts of the uniform seem to

have been extremely serviceable and certainly the men of Minnesota were renowned for their famous check or red shirts throughout the war. Some accounts about Minnesota troops as late as 1863 mention their broad hats and shirts. Officially the regular Army had long taken over supplying the Minnesota troops with uniforms by this time, but it seems that many men still treasured and maintained their early war uniforms.

At the outbreak of the Civil War Michigan's state authorities ordered that uniforms should immediately be made up of blue flannel or some other suitable material blue in colour. Many Michigan soldiers ended up wearing dark blue trousers and dark blue jackets which had standing collars like army regulation frock coats. The Michigan jackets had nine buttons down the front and shoulder straps. The men were also supplied with shirts, drawers, forage caps, socks, shoes, haversacks, canteens and cooking utensils, and the State also armed some of its soldiers with limited quantities of 1855 rifle muskets. The rest were largely armed with imported weapons.

On May 19 1861, New Jersey's State Board of Commissioners prescribed the uniform for the State's three month regiments as a 'dark blue frock coat, light blue pants and army cockade hat'. It appears that the dress the majority of New Jersey State troops wore would have differed very little from that of the regulars, except that their sack coats had five buttons down the front instead of four, but a feature of many officers' coats is that they were trimmed light blue down the front and on the cuffs. Unusually the State equipped two Zouave regiments, with their uniforms, and these had dark blue jackets, with dark blue waistcoats and trousers, a blue sash edged in light blue and blue and red forage caps.

Elite militia units in New Jersey could become part of the New Jersey Rifle Corps and wear either Chasseur pattern jackets or fatigue jackets. They could choose to wear either grey or blue Chasseur or fatigue jackets.

State issued buttons for New Jersey troops featured the New Jersey coat of arms although some buttons just had NJ stamped on them. New Jersey's arsenal at Trenton supplied many New Jersey troops with weapons, notably copies of the 1861 rifle musket.

Before the Civil War, Vermont hadn't provided any uniform regulations for its State troops and the rush to get volunteers into uniforms saw stocks of grey cloth being hastily ordered. The 1st Regiment Vermont Volunteers wore a dated looking grey uniform with tailed coats, but other regiments were outfitted in frock coats made out of brownish grey material trimmed in blue. The coats had nine buttons down the front and the trousers and forage caps issued to Vermont's volunteers early in the war were also distinctively trimmed in blue. State buttons bore the state coat of arms and Vermont underneath, and the 13th Vermont Regiment had special cap badges which featured the regimental number in a wreath. Arms issued to Vermont troops were a mixture of 1855 rifle muskets and smoothbore 1842 muskets.

The regular army eventually took over clothing supplies for Vermont regiments but it seems that instead of wearing comfortable sack coats Vermont troops preferred instead to wear regulation frock coats throughout the war as many pictures of Vermont troops show.

It seems that several States were lacking the means to outfit and equip their forces for the war. The worst offender was Ohio where the State arsenal contained little more than a few boxes of rusty smoothbore weapons, some of them more than 20 years old. It was even rumoured that some of these muskets dated as far back as the war of 1812. It would be a nightmare getting Ohio troops ready for war because the arsenal contained no accoutrements, not even basic items like belts or cartridge boxes.

It was a daunting task to make proper preparations but Ohio's Jacob D. Cox was determined that Ohio troops should be outfitted and armed properly. At the beginning of the Civil War, Ohio wanted to clothe her troops in uniforms that were so close to Army regulations that little change would be required when the troops went into U.S. service. However, the State wanted some part of the soldiers' uniforms to be distinctive, so it was recommended that the state coat of arms should be stamped on buttons and cap plates; but it seems that many of the troops just had regulation buttons on their clothing.

Before 1862, when the Federal authorities took over the task of uniforming Ohio's soldiers, Ohio arranged to outfit its troops by issuing clothing contracts to a number of firms both inside and outside the state. It was stressed that uniforms should be: 'thoroughly well made and trimmed and in all respects to conform to Regulations'. Ohio even contracted for a supply of 8,000 regulation infantry frock coats with brass shoulder scales, but supplies of blue cloth ran out and fresh stocks were difficult to procure.

Ohio infantry regiments had to be clad in less elaborate uniforms comprising blue flannel blouses, and sky blue kersey trousers. Blue fatigue caps with havelocks or glazed covers were given to troops and black felt hats were also issued, but these quickly lost their shape. Shirts were made out of red or grey flannel. Ohio's artillery and cavalrymen were issued with dark blue cloth shell jackets and dark blue reinforced trousers. Overcoats were of sky blue kersey.

Like many States, Ohio had troubles in getting enough supplies of blue wool, so uniforms were often made out of grey cloth instead and at least 10 Ohio regiments were uniformed in grey and more than 5,000 jackets made out of cadet grey cloth were issued. Late in the war, the Ohio State Militia was formed, a unit that wore uniforms identical to the Regular Army but which had state distinctions on waistbelts and cartridge box plates. Cartridge box plates and waistbelt plates were similar to regulation plates, but bore the initials 'OVM'. Circular shoulder belt plates bearing the 'OVM' initials were also worn.

Ohio regiments were armed with a bewildering array of weapons including 1842 smoothbore muskets converted from flintlock, Prussian muskets, and Enfield rifle muskets.

It was planned that all Pennsylvania regiments should be uniformly dressed in blue, but again sufficient quantities of blue material were impossible to obtain so grey uniforms were widely worn. Colours varied from cadet grey to tan or light grey and very dark grey. Some jackets which were made out of 'mixed forest cloth' were light grey on one side and dark grey on the other, making a very strange appearance.

Most Pennsylvania troops in the early days of the war would have worn grey forage caps, grey jackets and trousers. Jackets usually had nine or 12 buttons down the front and were looped at the bottom like many New York State jackets to keep waistbelts in place. Some troops also wore trousers of a linen material and even brown trousers were issued. A surprising number of Pennsylvania volunteer soldiers were still wearing grey uniforms even after 1862. The Philadelphia Home Guard wore grey uniforms for much of the war which must have looked very unusual when these grey uniforms were worn with full dress Hardee hats.

Many men of the Pennsylvania Reserve Corps formed from surplus regiments in the rush of men volunteering for Union service, were meant to wear regulation Union Army uniforms but many wore grey jackets and trousers. Buttons on Pennsylvania uniforms bore the state coat of arms and brass oval belt plates were also issued, often marked with individual unit designations. More often than not regulation army belt plates marked 'US' were worn. It doesn't seem that Pennsylvania had any trouble arming its men. Most of their weapons came directly from the government.

Illinois had very sparse dress regulations for its troops, merely requiring that volunteer officers should wear close approximations of the uniforms worn by regular officers in the Union Army. Illinois was hoping that the Federal government would arm and equip its men right from the start of the war, but the government was not forthcoming. Illinois troops at first received a sparse state issue of grey shirts, blue forage caps, and red blankets. The State authorities appear to have been so desperate for uniforms that a consignment of clothing was even ordered from suppliers in New York, but these uniforms which featured grey jackets and trousers and even Zouave caps, wore out very quickly.

When more regiments were raised in Illinois uniforms were locally made usually by seamstresses in the men's hometowns. Illinois soldiers could expect to receive grey or blue jackets and trousers but when the State made greater provisions for uniforms, volunteers were supposed to receive blue or grey jackets and trousers cut in the same style as U.S. regulation

Odd looking Whipple caps, like the one worn by this soldier were widely issued to troops from New York and New Hampshire. Despite their ungainly appearance, the hats proved to be popular. David Scheinmann.

jackets, two flannel shirts, two pairs of socks and a stout pair of shoes. In practice it seems that most Illinois volunteers wore grey uniforms with grey broad brimmed hats turned up at the side like regulation Hardee hats. Hats issued to a number of Illinois regiments featured the unusual ornamentation of a brass button attached to a red, white and blue cockade.

The 8th, 9th, 11th, and 12th infantry regiments in the first brigade of Illinois volunteers received grey coats edged in blue while artillery units received grey coats edge in red. Fatigue uniforms featuring Zouave caps were also issued. Cavalry regiments were issued with red shirts and dark blue trousers, but they were later issued with Union Army regulation dress. In 1862, doubtless much to the relief of State officials, the U.S. Quartermaster took over supplying Illinois troops with uniforms and a huge amount of uniform items were issued including more than 17,000 coats. Unlike the troops in many other States, Illinois soldiers are not thought to have worn any distinctive buttons with their uniforms. Illinois soldiers were mainly armed with Springfield rifle muskets.

Broad brimmed black hats originally issued to troops from Minnesota and Illinois were also a feature of the original State uniforms issued to volunteer soldiers from Indiana. Uniforms from Western States tended to be much more functional and far less decorative than the uniforms issued by their Eastern counterparts, largely because Western States didn't have such an old militia system as their Eastern comrades-in-arms. Regiments in Indiana were issued uniforms made out of satinet or jean cloth, the latter material is a form of cloth usually associated with uniforms manufactured in the Confederacy. Hats were meant to be looped up at each side.

It seems that two of Indiana's regiments began the war wearing grey jackets and trousers and blue shirts, while the others wore light blue jackets. In September 1861 grey uniforms trimmed with black were issued but it seems that when new regiments were raised they were outfitted in standard Army dress although many grey and blue jackets would have survived. Indiana's regiments received 1842 pattern smoothbore muskets and Enfield rifle muskets.

The State of Iowa took little pride in its militia units before the Civil War and at the outbreak of hostilities Iowa State authorities were forced to buy cloth from Chicago to make enough uniforms for Iowa troops. Some troops wore loose fitting baggy shirts with green trim and dark grey trousers, while others wore similar uniforms trimmed red, but these uniforms wore out in a matter of weeks. After the Battle of Wilson's Creek, Iowa troops were so destitute, that many were reduced to patching their trousers with material from flour sacks. Some even wore aprons made out of these sacks, because their trousers were beyond repair.

Replacement uniforms were ordered from Boston and these proved to be far sturdier. Troops from Iowa's first three infantry regiments were issued with grey frock coats and trousers, flannel shirts and felt hats. Later issues of clothing were made by the Federal government. Iowa troops were issued with a variety of weapons including French and Belgian rifles.

Wisconsin wanted its troops dressed in blue, but again there wasn't enough blue material to go around, so the majority of Wisconsin's volunteers wore grey uniforms. It was a particularly smart dress with single breasted frock coats, grey trousers ornamented with a black cord down each seam, grey kepis trimmed black and a grey overcoat with black piping.

The 3rd Wisconsin's uniform featured grey hunting shirts and light grey trousers. Other regiments wore single breasted jackets, with black shoulder straps and black decoration on the cuffs and collars. The jackets also had loops at the bottom so that a belt could be passed through and the rest of the uniform included grey forage caps, grey trousers with the popular black stripe down the seams and grey overcoats. Wisconsin volunteers were later largely dressed in blue uniforms issued by the State, including dark blue coats with stand up collars. Black hats, sky blue trousers and forage caps were also issued. Later in the war, Wisconsin regiments received their clothing from Federal supplies and were armed and dressed with regular uniforms, weapons and equipment.

Massachusetts had authorised a state uniform for its troops as far back as 1852, but many of its militia units were inadequately clothed at the beginning of the war. Many soldiers were just issued basic uniform parts such as shirts, but little else. Grey flannel uniforms were quickly made which came with red Zouave fezzes. This distinctive headgear was later replaced by felt hats, but doubtless many volunteers wore their fezzes for at least the first two years of the war. Massachusetts procured over 9,000 grey infantry jackets and over 1,000 cavalry and artillery jackets.

Two Massachusetts regiments never wore grey uniforms and were outfitted in blue right from the start of the war, and eventually all units from the State wore regulation blue. An interesting aspect of the accoutrements carried by Massachusetts volunteers is that many of them were British made. 10,000 British accoutrement sets were distributed to Massachusetts soldiers.

The dated long tailed coats that many New Hampshire Volunteers began the war in were considered to be out of step with uniform trends and they were replaced with state issued grey frock coats of a light or mid grey shade. Collar and cuffs were trimmed in red like the old coats, but the cuff trim like the regulation army frock coats was pointed. The coats had nine buttons down the front and the rear skirts of the coat were similar, if not identical to regulation frock coats.

The most distinctive part of New Hampshire's state issued uniforms was an unusual cap called a New Hampshire Cap that was similar to the unusual caps first issued but later rejected by Berdan's Sharpshooters. One New Hampshire soldier described his cap as: 'A helmet like structure of waterproof cloth with a visor before and behind, the top resembling a squash and the whole lined and padded. This was the

Opposite.

This corporal is also a New Hampshire Volunteer. David Scheinmann.

New Hampshire cap and although it would do in a row to keep blows from the head and was good to protect the neck from rain, yet in summer it was a sweltering concern.'

The hat visors were made out of leather, while the flaps at the back were made out of the same material as the main body of the caps. The caps had leather chin straps which were fastened with a buckle. New Hampshire troops were later provided with regulation dress that had a few subtle differences from standard Union Army uniforms. Frock coats did not have piping on the cuffs or collar and the shoulders had shoulder straps with pointed ends, held in place by a small button which didn't reach quite to the collar.

The famous blouses supervised by Ambrose E. Burnside for the 1st Regiment Rhode Island Detached Militia became the State's issued dress. Rhode Island had an array of individually clad militia units who wore different uniforms, many of them very dated. The Providence First Light Artillery who formed Companies C and D of the 1st Regiment wore scarlet tail coats trimmed light blue and buff with red and white epaulettes, light blue trousers with white stripes. The Pawtucket Light Guard, Company E of the same regiment wore a grey uniform trimmed yellow with red cuff flaps and a dress cap with a red pompon.

Surprisingly, it seems that Rhode Island's volunteers didn't mind swapping their elaborate uniforms for the more simple State outfits. Perhaps it was because their distinctive clothing picked up a lot of attention. The *Washington Star* wrote: 'Their dress is characteristic. At the bottom they wear stout, thick soled cowhide boots; their pants are homemade grey and over this they wear a dark blue jean frock or hunting shirt, added to which they mount the new army hat turned up at the side.' Officers wore variations of the standard blouse, some had five small buttons reaching down from the neck, some blouses had a large inside pocket, and some were double breasted.

The 1st Rhode Island Artillery Battery wore dress uniforms based on US Army regulations, which had dark blue frock coats and sky blue trousers. For fatigue dress enlisted men wore dark blue shell jackets piped in scarlet at the collar and cuffs and which had nine buttons down the front. Trousers were the standard reinforced issue. On campaign, officers wore dark blue Rhode Island blouses, dark blue trousers and forage caps. The second battery originally wore Rhode Island blouses and dress hats, but they were later issued with regulation light artillery dress.

Insignia and Medals

Ten years before the outbreak of the American Civil War, several changes were made to United States military insignia. Metal insignia for all branches of the service was cast in brass. Distinctive colours were also adopted for branches of service; blue for infantry, red for artillery and yellow or orange for the cavalry.

The yellow cavalry trim dated back to the dragoons' yellow trim authorised in 1833. At first, this trim clashed with the artillery who were already wearing yellow facings as their branch of service colour, and as some dragoon officers favoured wearing orange sashes, orange became the dragoons' branch of service colour. The cavalry in general adopted yellow when the facing colour of the artillery was changed to scarlet. Traditionally, the artillery had yellow as its facing colour, to match the yellow metal of its guns. But scarlet which had first been adopted by the American army in the Revolution was much more appropriate.

White facings had originally been adopted as the infantry's branch of service colour in 1832, but the infantry's facings were eventually changed to light blue or dark blue because the white cloth soiled too easily.

The War Department issued insignia which went on a soldier's accoutrements, while the ordnance department was largely responsible for issuing insignia which soldiers wore on their clothing. Some insignia has already been mentioned in this book, but the subject of Union insignia during the Civil War is so complex that it deserves a detailed study. One of the most distinctive forms of Union insignia was the eagle cap badge. Introduced in 1851, it was made out of gold embroidery for officers and yellow metal for enlisted men. The brass version featured a stamped design showing the United States national bird, the eagle. Eagle badges were slightly under $2^{1}/_{2}$ inches high and measured $1^{3}/_{4}$ inches between the wing tips.

Officers' eagles were richly embroidered in gold on an oval of black velvet fixed to a small tin plate which had two wire loops attached, so that the eagle could be fixed to the officer's headgear. There was no regulation for which way the eagle should look, eagles 'looking' both to the left and right were common.

Eagle symbols were also an important feature on officers' and NCOs' sword belt plates. In 1851 a new pattern for these plates was adopted that remained virtually unchanged until World War Two. Regulations stated that the belt plates should be: 'Gilt, rectangular, two inches wide with a raised rim, a silver wreath of laurel encircling the Arms of the United

The regulation embroidered bugle horn insignia is shown in this photograph of an officer holding his Hardee hat. David Scheinmann.

Rectangular belt plates like the one worn by the officer here, found much favour with cavalrymen. A brass eagle motif was surmounted by a silver wreath on these plates. David Scheinmann.

varied in design. Most were cast but others were stamped out of metal. Some had the silver wreath cast as an integral part of the plate but on many plates the wreaths were separate items added to the plates as a finishing touch.

Not only did officers of the 8th Wisconsin Infantry have eagle sword belt plates, the regiment actually carried a live eagle as part of its insignia. Bought from a Chippewa Indian, Old Abe the Battle Eagle was carried into battle tethered on top of a special perch and saw action several times, including the siege of Vicksburg in May 1863. Old Abe survived the war only to die of smoke inhalation when fire swept through the Wisconsin Capitol building where he spent his retirement.

Eagle plates used decoratively on shoulder belts supporting the infantryman's cartridge box, had a raised rim with an eagle holding three arrows and an olive branch. The plate itself was made out of stamped thin brass with a lead filled back with imbedded hooks for fastening it to the belt. The plates were also used to fasten the two halves of sergeants' shoulder belts together. Shoulder belt plates had a regulation diameter of 2.5 inches and while there were variations in design most shoulder belt plates followed a similar pattern.

Regulations stated that each infantryman should have an oval plate holding his waist belt together and another on the flap of his cartridge box. Classic U.S. plates dated as far back as the 1840s and came in two sizes; 3.5 by 2.2 inches and 2.8 by 1.6 inches. Usually the plates were made out of stamped brass filled with lead solder on the back. Most commonly they bore the letters US but many carried state initials.

Some of the most unusual cartridge box plates were the ones carried by the company of Zouaves raised by Captain H.T. Collis as a bodyguard for General Banks. These carried the initials 'Z.D.A.' standing for Zouaves d'Afrique. When the company was expanded to become the 114th Pennsylvania Volunteer Infantry, the men were issued with standard cartridge box plates, but some of the distinctive Z.D.A. plates probably saw service throughout the war.

Standard issue plates were made in Federal armouries, but more than 250,000 were also manufactured by private contractors. Circular brass two piece belt plates also saw service on white buff leather sword belts for carrying artillery swords or

States, eagle, shield scroll, edge of cloud and rays bright. The motto "E Pluribus Unum" in silver letters, upon the scroll, stars also of silver; according to pattern.'

Sword belts were attached to the plates usually by passing the right end of the belt through a slot in the right side of the plate. Despite regulations belt plates

Opposite.

As displayed on the forage cap of this officer, the infantry bugle horn insignia was one of the most widely worn during the Civil War. David Scheinmann.

This officer's crossed sabres are embroidered on a black piece of oval cloth. The number of his regiment and company letters also appear to have been added. David Scheinmann.

sabres.

In 1851, after years of unofficial use, insignia identifying infantry, cavalry and artillery were officially authorised. General officers and staff officers had an embroidered cap badge insignia with a silver 'U.S.' in old English characters in a golden laurel wreath. Cavalry insignia developed from the insignia worn by the old regiments of dragoons. The cap insignia

Enlisted men often displayed insignia on the tops of their forage caps, as shown here by these pipe smoking comrades. David Scheinmann.

authorised for the dragoons in 1851 was an orange pompom for enlisted men and crossed sabres for officers. The crossed sabres were in gold and had their edges upward. In the upper angle the regimental number was placed. This insignia was usually embroidered directly on to the cap, but crossed brass sabres began to become popular as well.

Enlisted men were later authorised to wear a brass company letter one inch high on their hats. When the dragoon regiments were authorised to wear felt hats in 1858, officers' insignia was worn on a black velvet background; an oval of velvet with a narrow embroidered border and tin backing. Enlisted men were now authorised to wear cross sabres, which came to be forever associated with the United States cavalry. Officers also continued to wear crossed sabres, either embroidered on black or blue cloth or in metal like their men.

The most distinctive Union infantry insignia was the bugle horn which was heavily influenced by the bugle horn insignia of the French voltigeurs. Bugle horn insignia had been adopted by the United States

This infantryman wearing an overcoat clearly displays the eagle buckle on his shoulder belt. David Scheinmann.

The most famous American insignia of all time are the cavalry's crossed sabres, here worn by a cavalry private. Such devices gave regiments valuable *esprit de corps*. David Scheinmann.

Army as early as 1831 but in 1851 the metal was changed from silver to gold and officers were authorised to wear a gold embroidered bugle on their caps within the number of their regiment in silver in the centre of the horn. Interesting variations on this are some Zouave officers who wore the letter 'Z' in the centre of the bugle horns on their kepis.

Some unique items of infantry insignia were the special cap plates worn by the 10th New York Volunteer Infantry, National Zouaves usually on the turbans wrapped around their fezzes. Not much is known about them, but they were over an inch long and were inscribed '10 NZ'. Infantrymen were specialists in arranging brass letters and numbers on their clothing and kepis. Many men of the 14th Brooklyn Regiment proudly bore the brass numerals 14 on the fronts of their kepis while the 11th New York often sported FZ letters standing for Fire Zouaves.

The distinctive castle insignia worn by the engineers and topographical engineers dated back to 1840 and it was used on the dress cap of U.S. Military Academy cadets in 1842. Engineer officers in the Civil War also wore an embroidered star within a laurel wreath on the collars of their coats. Apart from their distinctive buttons, officers of the topographical engineers also wore a gold embroidered shield surrounded by a wreath of oak leaves.

The ordnance department wore an embroidered shell and flame motif. Very much influenced by the French style, the Ordnance Department had worn its distinctive badges since 1833 and the unique design became exclusively theirs in 1851. Officers wore it in gold embroidery on their forage and dress caps, and embroidered in silver it was also worn on the crescents of their epaulettes. Enlisted men wore a similar design made out of brass on their caps and the collars of their uniforms, but eventually gave up wearing the device on their collars.

The famous crossed cannon of the artillery had been worn since 1833 and was officially adopted in 1851, when regulations stated that officers should wear gold embroidered badges with crossed cannon on their caps. They were also to have the regimental

This private of the 146th New York Volunteer Infantry, Garrard's Tigers, wears his corps badge on his chest. It was not unusual for men to make their corps badges out of wood or bone and also inscribe them with their name and the letter of their regimental company. Michael J. McAfee.

small circle of gold embroidery. Artillery officers' black velvet ovals were a little smaller than those worn by the cavalry. Miniature size cannon badges were also widely available and embroidered crossed cannon badges without the ovals were also widely worn.

Late in the Civil War, it seems that some horse artillery officers adopted a unique badge with a laurel wreath, a horse, crossed cannon and the words 'Horse Artillery'. Whether it was officially authorised or not isn't known and it represents just one of the many badge variations found in the Union Army.

Corps Badges

One of the most distinctive features of Union Civil War uniforms were the corps badges worn by soldiers on their forage caps or on their uniforms. Such badges gave soldiers a sense of identity and increased the esprit de corps of the Union Army. Unlike insignia or uniform regulations, the corps badge system was developed during the American Civil War and was unique to the conflict.

Corps badges were originated by Major General Philip Kearny as a means of identifying soldiers from a particular command after he mistakenly reprimanded some officers who were not under his direct orders. In May, 1862, Kearny ordered that the officers of his Third Division, Third Corps, Army of the Potomac, should sew a piece of red flannel 2 inches square on the fronts of their caps for identification purposes.

Legend has it that these badges, nicknamed 'Kearny patches' were cut from scarlet blankets bought by Kearny from France. Before the war Kearny had seen a lot of service with the French Army in North Africa and even charged with the French cavalry during one battle. Kearny was highly esteemd in the Union Army and when he was killed at the Battle of Chantilly in 1862, the distinctive red badges continued to be used as a tribute to him.

General Orders No 49, Headquarters of the 1st Division, Third Army Corps, issued to announce General Kearny's death, stated: 'To still further show our regard for him and to distinguish his officers as he wished, each officer will continue to wear on his cap a piece of scarlet cloth, or have the top or crown piece made out of scarlet cloth.' General Hooker widened the use of corps badges in a circular issued on March 21 1863, recommending the adoption of original corps badges 'for the purpose of ready recognition of corps and divisions of this army and to prevent injustice by

number in silver above the intersection of the cannon. These badges were also made in metal. Embroidered cannon badges came in different shapes and many featured different motifs but a common feature was the fact that the muzzle ends of the cannon designs were longer than the breech ends. Enlisted men had originally only been authorised to wear company letters in their caps, but in 1858 they were authorised to wear brass crossed cannon insignia with a brass regimental number and a company letter. The brass crossed cannon was reminiscent of the insignia worn on artillery dress caps before 1851, but the 1858 crossed cannon badges were flatter and had slimmer and longer cannon barrels. Like infantrymen, artillerymen put their badges and company letters either on the fronts of their forage caps, or on top.

In 1858 artillery officers' cap devices were changed to black velvet ovals of material bearing the gold embroidered cross cannon which also had the regimental number embroidered on a black base in a

Opposite.
This officer sports what looks to be a commercially available corps badge on the front of his frock coat. David Scheinmann.

Ogden painting of Union uniforms and corps badges. Peter Newark's Military Pictures.

reports of straggling and misconduct through mistake as to their organisations.'

Soon the entire Army was wearing corps badges. Union Corps were usually divided into three divisions and the colour of the badge corresponded to the number of the division. The 1st division wore red badges, the 2nd white, and the 3rd blue. When more than three divisions existed in a corps, green was used for the 4th and orange for the 5th.

Corps badges were also used on flags and also drawn on ambulances and wagons belonging to the particular corps. Regulations authorised that the 1st Army Corps should have a sphere symbol, the 2nd a trefoil, the 3rd a lozenge, the 4th an equilateral triangle, the 5th a Maltese cross and the 6th a Greek cross. The 7th Corps was discontinued before any orders for a badge were given and the 8th Corps unofficially used a star with six rays.

The 9th Corps saw duty in the south, east and west, and adopted a shield with a figure 9 as its badge. The centres of these badges also featured an anchor and a cannon. The 10th Corps spent a lot of its time building fortifications and a badge showing a four

bastioned fort was selected for it.

On March 21, 1863, a crescent was prescribed for the 11th Corps and the 12th Corps was to wear a 12 pointed star. When the Army of the Potomac was reorganised in March 1864 it was stipulated that transferred troops should preserve their badges. The combined 1st and 5th Corps used a circle surrounding a Maltese cross as their badge when the new 5th Corps was formed, while the 6th Corps retained a Greek cross.

The 13th Corps never had an official authorised badge during the war, but seems to have adopted an elipse shape surrounding a canteen. Corps serving in the Department of the Cumberland also had distinctive badges. General orders stated that they were 'For the purpose of ready recognition of the corps and divisions of this army and to prevent injustice by reports of straggling and misconduct through mistakes as to organisations.'

It was claimed the 14th Corps was given the distinctive acorn badge in memory of the bad times they went through in the autumn of 1863. The weather was so bad that supplies couldn't get through and the men were reduced to eating the acorns from a grove of oaks growing near their camp. Ingeniously, the men roasted and boiled the acorns and even ground them between stones to make bread. Not surprisingly, they were known ever after as the 'Acorn Boys'.

The 20th Corps, which was formed by consolidating the 11th and 12th Corps, adopted a five pointed star, the old badge of the 12th as its badge, but men of the 11th Corps jealously stuck to their crescent badges for a long time, using it in combination with the star.

The badge of the 15th Army Corps was described in general orders issued on February 15 1865: 'The following is announced as the badge of this corps: A miniature cartridge box, black, set transversely on a field of cloth or metal: above the cartridge box plate will be stamped or marked in a curve, the motto "Forty Rounds".'

This distinctive badge came about as a result of the rivalry between the Eastern soldiers of the 12th Corps and the Western soldiers of the 15th Corps. A soldier

Opposite.

Mary Tepe was awarded a Kearny Cross for her gallantry in action when she served as a vivandiere with the 114th Pennsylvania Volunteer Infantry Regiment, the Collis Zouaves. Based on the French idea, many Civil War Regiments had vivandieres who sold tobacco and liquor to the men and wore a version of their regiment's uniform. Michael J. McAfee.

This colonel wears a particularly large set of epaulettes. These uniform ornaments were favoured by the commanders of volunteer infantry regiments. David Scheinmann.

Infantry sergeant with chevrons. David Scheinmann.

of the 15th Corps joked that the star badges then carried by the 12th Corps made them all look like brigadiers, and when the 12th Corps men asked what the 15th Corps badge was he patted his cartridge box and said: 'this is the badge of the 15th Corps, 40 rounds.' The 15th Corps' commander, General Logan, later heard the story and this decided him on the 15th's corps badges.

No official order was ever given for a badge for the 16th Corps. Instead several designs were put into a hat and the first drawn out was accepted as the design for the corps badge. The rough drawing plucked out of the hat was a circle crossed by two bars at acute angles and this was modified into a figure resembling a Maltese cross with curved lines for the 16th Corps' badge. The badge was called the A.J. Smith Cross, in honour of the first commander of the corps.

The 17th Corps badge was an arrow design and though simple it was very memorable. In general orders issued on March 25, 1865, General F. P. Blake wrote: 'In its swiftness, in its surety of striking where wanted and in its destructive powers when so intended, the arrow is probably as emblematical of this corps as any design that could be adopted.'

The 18th Corps had a cross with foliated leaves as its badge, while the 19th Corps badge was changed from a four pointed star to a fan-leaved cross with an octagonal centre on November 17, 1864. Ironically the 19th hardly fired a hostile shot while they had this badge late in the war.

No official orders were ever made concerning badges for the 21st and 22nd Corps, but as the 22nd

Corps served in the defences of Washington, a pentagon was chosen with the edge cut into five equal sections and a circle in the centre. The 23rd Corps used a shield as its badge, while the 24th Corps, largely composed of veterans from the 10th and 11th Corps, adopted a heart as its badge in the closing stages of the war.

Orders dated March 18, 1865, explained the poignant feelings behind the choice of symbol: 'The symbol selected is one which testifies our affectionate regard for all our brave comrades - alike the living and the dead - who have braved the perils of this mighty conflict and our devotion to the sacred cause - a cause which entitled us to the sympathy of every brave and true heart and the support of every strong and determined hand.'

The 25th Corps composed of coloured soldiers from the 10th and 18th Corps had square corps badges, featuring a smaller square superimposed into the main design. These badges were very distinctive and when they were issued on February 20, 1865, General Weitzel had these words to say: 'Soldiers, to you is given a chance in this spring campaign, of making this badge immortal. Let history record that on the banks of the James thirty thousand freemen not only gained their own liberty, but shattered the prejudice of the world, and gave to the land of their birth peace, union and glory. '

The men of Hancock's First Corps, Veteran Volunteers, were never officially authorised a badge, but adopted badges with particularly elaborate motifs, which one account describes as: 'A circle is surrounded by a double wreath of laurel. A wide red band passes vertically through the centre of the circle. Outside the laurel wreath, rays form a figure with seven sides of concave curves. Seven hands, springing from the circumference of the laurel wreath, grasp spears, the heads of which form the seven points of the external radiated figure.'

Cavalry corps also adopted badges, even though no official orders were ever given authorising them. General J. E. Wilson's Cavalry Corps had a red swallow tailed cavalry guidon with crossed sabres suspended from a rifle or, alternatively, a carbine. The badge issued to Kilpatrick's Cavalry Corps had a swallow tail flag. It also had three gilt stars and an eagle motif. The Signal Corps badge had two flags crossed over the handle of a blazing torch, signifying that by day the signal corps used flags to signal, and by night they used torches.

Corps badges proved so popular that Union soldiers were given the legal right to wear them, even when they left the Army. Orders stated: 'All persons

On his unusual three button coat with pockets, this infantry first sergeant wears chevrons with a diamond shape above. David Scheinmann.

who have served as officers, non-commissioned officers, privates or other enlisted men in the Regular Army, volunteer or militia forces of the United States, during the war of the rebellion and have been honourably discharged from the service, or still remain in the same, shall be entitled to wear, on occasion of ceremony, the distinctive army badge ordered for or adopted by the army corps and division respectively in which they served.'

Epaulettes
American officers had traditionally worn epaulettes as a badge of rank and although their use was beginning to die out in the early years of the Civil War, it was not unusual to find them particularly on the shoulders of some militia officers. The 69th New York State Militia had worsted epaulettes on its new jackets adopted shortly before the war. These epaulettes had a broad bullion fringe for NCOs, a medium fringe for sergeants, and a narrow fringe for corporals and privates.

Epaulettes were expensive uniform accessories and

were individually tailored to fit the left and the right shoulder. Epaulettes were fixed on the shoulder by an open brass strap on the underside which passed through cloth loops on the wearer's shoulder and were secured by a spring clip. Epaulettes came with three sizes of bullion fringe. For general and field officers the fringe was 3.5 inches long and .5 of an inch in diameter, for captains it was 2.5 inches long and .25 inch in diameter and for lieutenants it was the same length. Colonels had a silver embroidered eagle on their epaulettes, lieutenant colonels had a silver embroidered oak leaf, captains had two silver embroidered bars and first lieutenants had one silver embroidered bar.

The cost of epaulettes helps to explain their declining use and why they were usually reserved for full dress occasions. Replacing epaulettes for widespread use were shoulder straps and these came in a regulation size of 1.375 by four inches. Shoulder straps all had gold embroidery trim on the borders and regulations stipulated that the borders should be .25 inches in width; but many officers bought shoulder straps which had wider borders. Originally, shoulder strap borders were sewn on cloth designating the branch of service the officer belonged to. The rank indications on shoulder straps were the same as for epaulettes.

Prior to the Civil War, worsted epaulettes were worn by enlisted men in all branches of the Army. Artillerymen wore scarlet epaulettes, and infantry light or Saxony blue. Enlisted men's epaulettes had crescents made out of worsted cord and straps made out coarse material attached to a piece of tin plate. The epaulettes had three rows of fringes which were three inches long often held in place at the bottom by a cord running through the ends. Epaulettes were fastened to the men's coats by a hook at the pointed end of the strap and a loop of cloth on each shoulder which the strap could be passed through.

Worsted epaulettes were eventually withdrawn and replaced by brass scales which had previously only been worn by cavalrymen as shoulder protectors and can be regarded as the last vestiges of medieval armour. Scales were called different names. 1851 regulations called them shoulder knots, which was a little peculiar because they didn't resemble shoulder knots at all, but they were usually officially called 'shoulder straps (brass)' or 'metallic scales'. The scales were originally issued in two patterns, one for non-commissioned staff and the other for dragoons and light artillery.

Brass scales issued to privates had seven scalloped pieces of metal, mounted on a strap which was slightly over two inches wide with a rounded end and four inch wide crescent. Sergeants' scales were similar in design, but their crescents were slightly larger and the scales and six of the scallops each had three small round head rivets. The scales were attached to soldiers' coats by open brass straps that were fixed to cloth or brass straps on the shoulders and over brass staples near the collar.

Chevrons

The French Army had originally introduced chevrons in the mid-18th century as a mark of long service for soldiers. The British adopted chevrons as badges of rank in 1802 and the American Army began using them shortly after the end of its second war with Britain in 1817. Chevrons were first worn by cadet military officers at the West Point Military Academy and in 1821 the United States Army authorised them to be worn by commissioned and non-commissioned officers. Around 1830, chevrons were banned for officers and from then on were worn by non-commissioned officers only.

A proper chevron system in the United States Army began in 1851. With some exceptions like the chevrons worn by United States Marines, chevrons pointed down and were in the cloth of the sergeant's branch of service. They were worn on the upper arms and had a small space between the seams. Diagonal pattern half chevrons were also authorised to be worn on the lower sleeves marking each period of five year service a soldier may have attained.

In the Civil War, these chevrons were issued to soldiers whose terms of service had expired but who had re-enlisted voluntarily in the army for another tour of duty. Sometimes these veterans wore their chevrons in the shape of an inverted V on their left coat sleeves.

Sergeant majors' chevrons were three stripes with an arc of three stripes above. Regimental quartermaster sergeants had three stripes and a tie of three stripes, ordnance sergeants had three stripes and a star, first sergeants had three stripes and a lozenge, sergeants had three stripes and corporals had two stripes. Sergeants and corporals of the 5th New York, Duryée's Zouaves, had particularly gaudy chevrons, with gilt on the stripes.

Opposite.

The epaulettes worn by this cavalry or artillery sergeant do not have shoulder scales but appear to be cloth boards with metal crescents and worsted fringes. They are certainly non-regulation. David Scheinmann.

Parrott rifle gun used in American Civil War. Peter Newark's Military Pictures.

Union Artillery, Malvern Hill, July 1862.

The painting opposite shows one of the gun crews in the massed Union Artillery at Malvern Hill, lined up to fire across an open plain about 400 yards wide, which proved to be devastating against Confederate troops woefully under-supported by their own artillery in this battle.

Unlike the variety of uniforms found in the Confederate Artillery, such as the Washington Artillery of New Orleans who began the war wearing blue frock coats, there was never the same variety of dress with Union field artillery. Ramming home a charge in the Napoleon cannon, the artilleryman, in the centre of the picture, wears a typical artillery shell jacket trimmed red. Artillerymen were also proud of the red stripe on their regulation kersey trousers. Other crew members are dressed similarly, but in the background an artilleryman can be seen in his waistcoat and shirtsleeves. Firing and moving artillery pieces rated amongst some of the most strenuous work on the battlefield and it was not unusual for artillerymen to remove their jackets in the heat of combat.

The days of the light artillerymen's spectacular looking Ringgold caps are long gone. Such elaborate headgear would have proved impractical when moving cannon around and the men in this picture wear ordinary forage caps with brass crossed cannon insignia marking their branch of service. Like the infantry, a considerable variety of kepis and slouch hats would be found in an average artillery regiment.

In the event of their battery being overrun artillerymen were often extremely vulnerable. A short sword, which looked like the swords carried by Roman Legionnaries, had been adopted for artillery in 1832 and was regulation until 1870, but they never saw widespread use in the Civil War. Officers carried ordinary swords, but enlisted men would have little to fight back with, apart from their artillery rammers and any other pieces of equipment that quickly came to hand.

The artillery officer on horseback wears a regulation frock coat and his kepi has gold embroidered crossed cannon insignia. Many artillery batteries during the war were short of men and in some cases made do with hastily trained infantrymen who either volunteered or who were pressed into service. The Union artillery may not have had the same panache that it developed before the War and its uniforms might not have had quite the same character, but it performed admirably. Painting by Chris Collingwood.

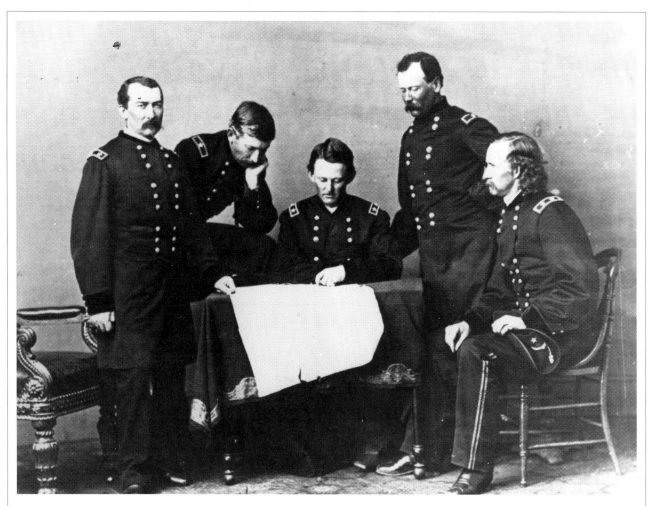

General Philip Henry Sheridan (standing extreme left) holding war conference with his officers. General George Armstrong Custer sits extreme right. Peter Newark's Military Pictures / M. Brady.

Aiguilettes

Aiguilettes, twisted strands or metallic cord or braid, were popular with some officers. Usually they were made out of twisted gold or silver and were suspended from the right shoulder under the epaulette. Aiguilettes had a practical as well as a decorative use, the ends sometimes contained pencils which meant officers could conveniently take notes or write out orders in the field. Regulations never prescribed the wearing of aiguilettes and they usually had to be privately purchased.

Baldrics

Baldrics were leather shoulder belts carried by some officers. They were often festooned with gold lace and a lion's head usually of gilded brass was fixed to the front. Three brass chains were suspended from the lion's mouth with pins on the end that fitted behind a shield made out of the same metal. Suspended by rings from the belt was a small brass mounted leather box. The length of the belt was adjusted by a brass buckle with a brass tip and loop and the purpose of the baldric was purely ornamental. Baldrics had originated in the 16th Century when the boxes were used to hold cartridges and the pins were used to clear out the touch holes of muzzle loading pistols.

Medals

On the eve of the Civil War, the Union didn't have a medal for gallantry. The first such medal issued was the Medal of Honor authorised by President Lincoln on December 21, 1861, and authorised by Congress on July 12, 1862. The first recipient of this medal was Corporal Francis Edward Brownell of the 11th New York Fire Zouaves, for his action in gunning down a Virginia tavern keeper James T. Jackson who shortly before had shot the Fire Zouaves' leader Elmer E. Ellsworth dead, after Ellsworth had removed a Confederate flag flying from the roof of the Marshall House tavern in Alexandria.

Brownell's action wasn't exactly a great act of bravery, but in the wave of grief that swept across the

Opposite.

Thomas Francis Meagher, wears an ornamental baldric in this picture. His green frock coat was one of the several dazzling outfits he appeared in throughout the war. David Scheinnman.

Andrew Scott, a freed save who served in the Union Army.
Peter Newark's Military Pictures.

The heroic actions of Major Robert Anderson and the men who defended Fort Sumter were the inspiration for the creation of a medal. David Scheinmann.

North after Ellsworth's demise, it was certainly a smart, politically correct move, to award him with a medal.

The Army Medal of Honor was similar to the Medal of Honor struck for the Navy, except that the Union Army's medal was attached to its ribbon by an American eagle and a crossed cannon. The Navy's had an anchor and a star.

The Medal of Honor hung from a ribbon which had 13 alternating stripes of red and white with a solid blue stripe running across the top and it was attached to a small shield. The medal featured a five pointed bronze star and on the obverse was a female warrior representing the Union, holding back an attacker carrying writhing snakes with her shield.

During the Civil War many other medals were officially proposed. The Sumter Medal, issued by the New York State Chamber of Commerce was given to the men who had defended Union Fort Sumter at the beginning of the war and more than 100 were awarded. The Butler medal for coloured Troops was awarded to black soldiers in the 25th Corps for gallantry displayed in the storming of New Market

Heights and at the Battle of Chaffins' Farm in 1864. 200 of these medals were issued and today they are very collectable.

Kearny Medals, named after General Philip Kearny were awarded to officers and men who had served with distinction in the late General's command. The medals had a gold medal cross and an inscription in Latin and more than 300 men received them. The Kearny Cross, another medal named after the popular general, was awarded as a cross of valour by Kearny's successor Brigadier General D. B. Birney. Kearny Crosses supplemented Kearny Medals and it was ruled that soldiers could not receive both medals. The medals, which were cast in bronze, were inscribed Kearny Cross on one side and Birney's Division on the other.

Opposite.
Fire Zouave corporal Francis Brownell was awarded the Congressional Medal of Honor for gunning his commander's killer down. Here Brownell wears the Fire Zouaves' first style of uniform. Peter Newark's Military Pictures.

Bibliography

Main Sources

U.S. Army Dress Regulations, William H. Horstmann & Sons, Philadelphia, 1851.

Todd F, P., *American Military Equipage 1851-1872* Volume I, Volume II, Volume III. The Company of Military Historians, West Brook Connecticut 1978. Separate Volume on State Forces published 1983.

Andrews, H., Nelson, C., Pohanka, B., Roach, H., *Photographs of American Civil War Cavalry*, Guidon Press, Pennsylvania 1982.

Carter, S., *The Last Cavaliers*, St Martin's Press, New York, 1979.

Davis, William C., *The Fighting Men Of The American Civil War*, Salamander Books 1989.

Downey F., *Sound Of The Guns*, David McKay Company Inc 1956

Downey F., *Clash Of Cavalry, The Battle of Brandy Station*, Butternut Press, Gaithersburg, Maryland 1985.

Echoes Of Glory: Arms & Equipment of the Union, TimeLife Books 1991.

Griffith, P. J., *Rally Once Again*, The Crowood Press 1987.

Herr, J. K., and Wallace, E. S., *The Story Of The U.S. Cavalry 1775-1942*, Bonanza Books, New York, 1981.

Military Uniforms In America, Long Endure: The Civil War Period 1852-1867, The Company Of Military Historians, Presidio Press, Novato, California 1982.

Lord, F A., *Civil War Collector's Encyclopedia*, Castle Books, New York 1965.

Lord, F. A., *They Fought For The Union*, Bonanza Books.

Naisawald. L. V. Loan., *Grape And Canister, The Story Of The Field Artillery Of The Army Of The Potomac.* Zenger Publishing Co, Washington D.C. 1983.

McAfee M. J., *Zouaves The First And The Bravest*, Thomas Publications, Gettysburg, Pennsylvania, 1991.

The Photographic History Of The Civil War, The Cavalry, edited by Theo E. Rodenbough, The Fairfax Press, New York 1983.

Sylvia S.W. & O'Donnell M. J., *The Illustrated History of American Civil War Relics*, Moss Publications, Orange Virginia, 1978.

Troiani D., Pohanka B., *Don Troiani's Civil War*, Stackpole Books, Mechanicsburg Pennsylvania, 1995

Urwin G.J.W., *The United States Infantry, An Illustrated History 1775-1918*, Blandford Press 1988.

Urwin G.J.W., *The United States Cavalry, An Illustrated History*, Blandford Press 1983.

Warren R., Federal Data Series No 1. *1st To 5th New Hampshire Volunteer Infantry 1861-1862*, Confederate Historical Society 1987.

Warren R., Federal Data Series No 2: *1st Rhode Island Detached Militia, 2nd Rhode Island Volunteer Infantry, 1st and 2nd Rhode Island Batteries 1861*, Confederate Historical Society 1987.

Warren R., Federal Data Series No 2: *Uniforms And Flags Of The 69th New York State Militia And The Irish Brigade 1859-1865*, Confederate Historical Society Press 1988.

Windrow M., Embleton G., *Military Dress Of North America 1665-1970*, Ian Allen Ltd, 1973.

Zimmerman, R. J., *Unit Organizations of the American Civil War*, Rafm Co Inc, Ontario, Canada, 1982

The Image of War 1861-1865, Vol I Shadows Of The Storm, Editor William C Davis, National Historical Society, Gettysburg, Pennsylvania, Doubleday & Company Garden City, New York, 1981.

The Image Of War 1861-1865, Vol VI The End Of An Era, Editor William C. Davis, National Historical Society, Gettysburg, Pennsylvania, Doubleday & Company Garden City, New York, 1984

Griffith, P., *Battle In The Civil War*, Fieldbooks, 1986

Katcher P., *Fotofax Union Forces of the American Civil War*, Arms & Armour Press, London 1989.

Kinsley D.A. *Favor the Bold, Custer The Civil War Years*, Promontory Press, 1967.

Urwin, G.J.W. *Custer Victorious The Civil War Battles of General George Armstrong Custer*, Associated University Presses East Brunswick, New Jersey, 1983

Coggins J., *Arms And Equipment Of The Civil War*, Doubleday and Company Inc, Garden City, New York, 1962.

Cunliffe, C., *Soldiers And Civilians The Martial Spirit In America 1775-1865*, Eyre & Spottiswoode, London 1968.

Wright S.J. *The Irish Brigade, Combat History Series, The Civil War*, Steven Wright Publishing, Springfield, Pennsylvania, 1992.

Regimental Histories

Brainard, M.G., *Campaigns of the One Hundred and Forty Sixth Regiment New York State Volunteers*, New York, 1915.

Conyngham D.P., *The Irish Brigade And Its Campaigns*, Patrick Donahoe, Boston, 1869. Reprinted by Ron R.

Van Sickle Military Books, Gaithersburg, Maryland, 1987.

Cowtan C.W., *Services of the 10th New York Volunteers (National Zouaves) in the War of the Rebellion*, Charles & Ludwig, New York, 1862.

Davenport A., *Camp and Field Life of the Fifth New York Volunteer Infantry Duryee Zouaves*, Dick and Fitzgerald, New York, 1879. Reprinted by the Butternut Press, Gaithersburg, Maryland, 1984.

Dowley M.E., *History and Honorary Roll of the Twelfth Regiment*, New York, 1869

Glover, E.A., *Bucktailed Wildcats, A Regiment of Civil War Volunteers*, Thomas Yosseloff, New York & London, 1960.

Johnson C.F., *The Long Roll, Impressions Of A Civil War Soldier*, Elbert Hubbard, East Aurora New York 1911. Reprinted by Carabelle Books, Shepherdstown, West Virginia 1986.

Jones P., *The Irish Brigade*, Robert B Luce Inc, Washington & New York, 1960.

Nash E.A., *A History of the Forty Fourth Regiment New York Volunteer Infantry*, Chicago 1911. Reprinted by the Morningside Bookshop, Dayton Ohio 1988

Nolan A.T., *The Iron Brigade, A Military History*, Indiana University Press, 1994.

Ripley W.Y.W., *Vermont Riflemen In The War For the Union 1861 To 1865 A History of Company F First United States Sharp Shooters*, Tuttle & Co 1883. Reprinted by the Grand Army Press, Rochester, Michigan, 1981.

The 155th Regimental Association, *Under the Maltese Cross Antietam to Appomattox*, Pittsburgh 1910.

Roehrenbeck W.J., *The Regiment That Saved The Capital*, Thomas Yosselof, London & New York 1961.

Tevis W.C. *The History of The Fighting Fourteenth*, New York 1911.

Magazine Sources

Bender D., Boots and Saddles, 'A Survey of the U.S. Cavalry from the Civil War to the Great War',

Military Images, West Chester Pennsylvania, 1985, Volume VIII, No. 1 pp. 2021.

Field R., 'American Lancers', *Military Illustrated*, London, 1995, No. 91, pp. 2429.

Field R.,'American Hussars', *Military Illustrated*, London, 1996, No. 93, pp. 3035.

Karle T., 'The 83rd Pennsylvania Volunteer Infantry 18611862', *Military Images*, West Chester, Pennsylvania, 1990, Volume XII NO. 1, pp. 2729.

Marcot R. M. 'The Uniforms & Field Equipment of the Berdan U.S. Sharpshooters', *North South Trader's Civil War*, Orange Virginia, 1990, Volume XVII NO. 6, pp. 2840.

McAfee M.J., 'The Well Accoutered Soldier, Army Uniforms of the Civil War Part IX', *Military Images*, West Chester, Pennsylvania, 1988, Volume X, NO. 1, pp. 1824.

McAfee M.J.,'Empire State Soldiers, Images From New York's Bureau of Military Statistics', *Military Images*, West Chester, Pennsylvania, 1990, Volume X1, NO. 4, pp. 1625.

Osborne S.R., 'They Wore An Orange Ribbon', *Military Collector & Historian Westbrook*, Connecticut, 1986, Volume XXXVIII, NO. I, pp. 4042.

Pohanka B., 'Like Demons With Bayonets, The 5th New York Zouaves at Gaines's Mill', *Military Images*, West Chester, Pennsylvania, 1989, Volume X NO. 6, pp. 1222.

Rossbacher N., 'Identification Discs & Inscribed Corps Badges', *North South Trader's Civil War*, Orange, Virginia, 1990, Volume XVII No. 5, pp. 2431.

Smith R., 'The Magnificent Zouaves, 5th New York Volunteer Infantry 1861-1863,' *Military Illustrated*, London, 1994, No. 78, pp. 1417.

Smith R., 'Red Legged Devils, 14th Brooklyn Regiment', *Military Illustrated*, London 1995, No. 86, pp. 2528.

Warren R., '11th New York Volunteer Infantry, Ellsworth's First New York Fire Zouaves 18611862, *Military Collector & Historian*, Westbrook, Connecticut, 1987, Volume XXXIX No. 4, pp. 174177.

Urwin G.J.W., 'Come On You Wolverines Custer's Michigan Cavalry Brigade', *Military Images*, West Chester, Pennsylvania, Volume VIII NO 1 pp. 716.

Civil War Directory

This directory is a comprehensive guide for American Civil War re-enactors, Civil War historians, art collectors, modellers and wargamers.

American Re-enactment Groups

Big battle re-enactments in America can boast upwards of 6,000 troops. At the Gettysburg anniversary reenactment in 1988 over 14,000 men took part. Many British reenactors travel to the States during the summer to take part with members of American reenactment groups. The following is a list of some of the hundreds of groups in the States.

5th New York Volunteer Infantry, Duryee's Zouaves. Contact: P.O. Box 1601 Alexandria VA 22313. The 5th New York is one of the oldest reenactment units in the States and its captain is the noted American Civil War historian, Brian Pohanka. During the American Civil War, the original 5th New York boasted dozens of Englishmen in its ranks, some of them Crimean War veterans.

28th Massachusetts Volunteer Infantry. Contact: Guy Morin, PO Box 108, Auburn MA 01501. Phone: 5088323175.

48th New York Volunteer Infantry. Contact: Lou Evans, 1321 Hammerhead Lane, Virginia Beach VA 234646326.

111th Pennsylvania Volunteer Infantry Company I. Contact: Patrick A. Tarasovitch, 9800 Mark Road, Erie, PA 16509.

28th Pennsylvania Volunteer Infantry, Company C. Contact: Andy Waskie, G.A.R. Museum. 4278 Griscom Street, Philadelphia, PA 19124. Phone: 215-2896484.

56th Pennsylvania Volunteer Infantry. Contact: 1st Sergeant Grehl, RR 6 Box 6394E, Stroudsburg, PA 18360.

9th New York Heavy Artillery. Contact: Frank Cutler, 6343 Kelly Road, Sodus, NY 14551. Phone: 3154839254.

76th Pennsylvania, Keystone Zouaves. Contact: Mike Deem, 437 Corona Drive, Morgantown WV 26505.473

2nd Maine Cavalry. Contact: Major Bunker, 903 Anne Street Wharf, Baltimore MD 21231. Phone: 4102768220

81st Pennsylvania Volunteer Infantry, Company K. Contact: Theodore P. Dombroski, 768 McNair Street, Hazleton, PA 182021.

46th Illinois Volunteer Infantry. Contact: Andy Gelman, P.O. Box 1022, Highland Park, Il 60035. Phone: 708 8312648.

119th New York Volunteer Infantry Company H. Contact: Joe Billardello, P.O. Box 184, Manorville, NY 11949.

1st New Jersey Artillery Battery B. Contact: Greg Putman, 18A Anbrey Street, Summit, NJ. Phone: 201535 3745.

1st Regiment Berdan's Sharpshooters, Company B. Contact: Thomas Carton 9147829497 or John Carey 5166667348. This group is mainly based in the New York, New Jersey and Pennsylvania areas.

14th New Jersey Volunteer Infantry, Co. K. Contact: 14th NJ Volunteers P.O. Box 646 Dayton NJ 08810 or phone Steve Milek on 9085212329.

8th Michigan Volunteer Infantry, Co C. Contact: Terry McKinch, 7432 East Potter Road, Davison MI 48423.

15th New York Volunteer Cavalry, Co L. Contact: John Milteer 914 6925902.

46th Illinois Volunteer Infantry. Contact: 46th IVI P.O. Box 921, Joliet Il. 604340921.

2nd New Jersey Volunteer Cavalry, Co A. Contact; Bill Anania, P.O. Box 673, Middletown, N.J. 07748. Phone: 9086711546.

9th Pennsylvania Reserves Co A. Contact: Bob Luther, 137 Fieldgate Drive, Pittsburgh PA 15241.

1st Minnesota Volunteer Infantry Co D. Contact: James D Owens, 1639 Belvedere Boulevard, Silver Spring MD 20902.

24th Michigan Volunteer Infantry. Contact: 604

Linden Street, Big Rapids MI49307. Phone: 6167960747. 700

83rd Pennsylvania Volunteer Infantry. Contact: Robert F. Frazier, 5511 Partridge Court, Harrisburg PA 17111. Phone 717 7877111 during the day, or 7176571717 in the evenings.

Co. B Tiger Rifles, (Wheat's Tigers). Contact Peter Leccese, 9137 85th Street, Woodhaven NY 11421. Phone: 7182965897.

19th Virginia Volunteer Infantry. Contact: R. Mason, 14204 Radford Court, Woodbridge VA 22191.

1st Regiment Virginia Volunteers, Co D. Contact: Bob Lyons,15 Highfields Drive, Baltimore, MD 21228. Phone: 4107473271.

21st Mississippi Volunteers Co H. Contact: John J. Wrona,363 Quaker Highway, Uxbridge MA01569. PHone: 5082786056.

21st Virginia Volunteers Co F. Contact: Floyd Bane, 14407 Huntgate Woods Road, Midlothian VA VA 23112. Phone: 8042317852.

3rd Arkansas. Contact: Denis on 8043631903 or Terry on 7179393629.

1st Virginia Cavalry. Contact: Nick Nichols, HCR 3, Box 378A, Rochelle, VA 22736. Phone: 7039486879.

13th North Carolina Troops. Contact Rex Hovey: 9225 Surrey Road, Mint Hill NC 28227. Phone: 7045459760.

21st Regiment, North Carolina Troops. Contact: Clark Fox, 410 Keating Drive, Winston Salem NC 27104.

51st North Carolina Volunteer Infantry. Contact: Mike Murley, 910 4256836 or Mike Carraway 910 424 3963.

19th Virginia Volunteer Infantry, Co K. Contact: Ken Thaiss, 10 Carriage Way, Freehold, NJ 07728. Phone 9087804802. Fax: 9087804803.

30th Virginia Volunteer Infantry. Contact: Bruce Drummond, 6 Oakcrest Court, East Northport, NY 11731. Phone: 5167541918.

55th Virginia Volunteer Infantry. Contact: Eugene Tucceri,38 Beverley Heights, Middletown, CT 06457. Phone: 2033475750.

45th Alabama Volunteer Infantry/18th Missouri Volunteer Infantry. Contact: Mark Hubbs, 2054649751.

58th Virginia Infantry. Contact: Chris Loving, 7037240974.

1st Tennessee Volunteer Infantry, Co B. Contact: Ed Sharp, 12211 Amy Dee Lane, Medway, Ohio 45341.

7th Tennessee Volunteer Infantry. Contact: Sergeant Howard, 6096253233.

British Re-enactment Groups

In Britain, the two main umbrella organisations for American Civil War re-enactment groups are the Southern Skirmish Association, Soskan, and the American Civil War Society the A.C.W.S. For information about joining Soskan write to, The Secretary, Southern Skirmish Association, PO Box 485, Swindon SN2 6BF. As this book went to press Soskan had the following Northern Southern units, for prospective recruits to choose from.

2nd U.S. Artillery Battery A
2nd U.S. Sharpshooters
2nd U.S. Cavalry
18th Missouri
28th Massachusetts
42nd Pennsylvania
1st Minnesota Infantry
1st Minnesota Artillery
79th New York Veteran Reserve
6th Pennsylvania Cavalry

1st Arkansas
15th Arkansas
9th Kentucky
16th Tennessee
Palmetto Sharpshooters
4th Virginia
7th Virginia Cavalry
17th Virginia
23rd Virginia
Confederate Artillery
Virginia Medical Department

For information about the A.C.W.S. write to PO Box 52, Brighouse, West Yorkshire, HD6 1JQ and you can be put in touch with one of the following Northern/ Southern units

2nd U.S. Infantry
24th Michigan
2nd Wisconsin
19th Indiana
14th Brooklyn
69th New York
2nd U.S. Artillery Battery B

The 24th Michigan can also be contacted directly by writing to Mark Gregory 82 Brierly Street, Bury, Lancashire BL9 9HW. Phone: 01617052433.

32nd Virginia Infantry
1st Tennessee Infantry
43rd Borth Carolina Infantry
43rd North Carolina Infantry
2nd South Carolina Infantry
13th Mississippi Infantry
4th Texas Infantry
1st Louisiana Zouaves
Washington Artillery of New Orleans
Virginia Artillery

55th Virginia
Widely acclaimed as Britain's finest American Civil War reenactment group, the 55th Virginia Infantry is an independent unit and not a member of either Soskan or the A.C.W.S. The 55th is noted for the excellence of its drill displays, authentic dress, accoutrements, and encampments. For information write to: Richard O'Sullivan, Flat 11, Grove Lodge, Crescent Grove, Clapham Common, London SW4 7AE. Phone: 01716224109.

Civil War Re-enactment Suppliers

The growth in living history and battle reenactments over the past few years has led to a steady growth of specialist equipment suppliers in Britain and America, who can satisfy reenactment requirements from a forage cap to a tent peg.

Britain's largest supplier of American Civil War reenactment equipment including haversacks, cap pouches, cartridge boxes, buttons and buckles is Alan Thrower who runs The Sutler's Store, 16 Howlett Drive, Hailsham East Sussex, BN27 1QW.

Many British American Civil War reenactors buy their clothing from companies in America. Some of the best Civil War uniforms renowned for their correct cut and colour are manufactured by Charlie Childs. Charlie runs his company County Cloth from 13797C, Georgetown Street NE, Paris Ohio, 44669.

America's oldest established American Civil War reenactment clothing supplier is the C & D Jarnagin Company P.O. Box 1860, Corinth MS 38834. Phone: 6012871977. Fax: 601 287 6033. Apart from complete uniforms Jarnagin also specialises in leather gear, footwear and tinware.

Other American firms manufacturing reproduction uniforms include Confederate Yankee P.O. Box 192,

Guilford CT 06437. Phone: 2034539900. Centennial General Store, 230 Steinwehr Avenue, Gettysburg PA 17325. Phone: 7173349712.

Civil War A frame tents and shelter halves are available from Panther, 1,000 P.O. Box 32, Normantown, WV 25267. Phone 3044627718.

American Civil War Organisations

The American Civil War Round Table (UK) is Britain's leading Civil war study group and one of hundreds of American Civil War Round tables around the world. The American Civil War Round table (UK) has members all over Britain and regular meetings are held, usually in London. For further information contact, Tony Daly, 57 Bartlemas Road, Oxford OX4 1XU. Tel: 01865201216.

The Military Order of the Loyal Legion of the United States is open to direct and collateral descendants of commissioned officers of the Union Army and was founded in 1865. For information contact Robert G. Carroon, 23 Thompson Road, West Hartford, Connecticut, 01072535.

Sons Of Union Veterans of the Civil War is open to male descendants of Civil War soldiers. Write to S.U.V.C.W. 1310 Forest Park Avenue, Dept TC, Valparaiso, IN 46383.

Heritagepac is a national lobbying group dedicated to preserving American battlefields against business concerns who want to turn battlesites into shopping malls or housing developments. For information write to P.O. Box 7281, Little Rock AR 72217.

The Save Historic Antietam Foundation is aimed at preserving one of America's most important Civil War battle sites. For information contact SHAF at P.O. Box 550, Sharpsburg, MD 21782. Phone: 3014322522.

The Bucktail Regimental Association studies and celebrates the men of Pennsylvania's famous Bucktail regiments. For information contact Major Richard Miller, 1405 Blue Mountain Parkway, Harrisburg, PA 17112. Phone 7175459830.

The Fourteenth Brooklyn Regiment, New York State Militia Society of New York Inc, preserves the memory of the famous Red legged devils, one of the most outstanding regiments of the Civil War. Write to Morton Berger, 2978 Ave. 'W' Apt 2A Brooklyn N.Y. 11229 for details. Mr Berger is the society's historian and curator of the 14th Brooklyn's armoury.

The Ulysses S. Grant Network promotes the study of the fabled Union general. Write for details to Donna Noralich, 238 Morse Avenue, Wyckoff N.J. 07481 USA.

The Company Of Military Historians has published many articles and plates on American Civil War regiments and its international membership boasts the cream of Civil War scholars. For details write to The Company of Military Historians, North Main Street, CT 06498 USA.

The Sons of Confederate Veterans is open to descendants of men who fought for the South during the Civil War. For information write to Arthur Kuydenkall Jr, 193 Clover Ridge Ct, Edgewater Florida, 32141, USA.

The John Pelham Historical Association celebrates the life and times of the South's finest horse artillery commander. For membership details write to Peggy Vogtsberger, 7 Carmel Terrace, Hampton VA 23666, USA. Phone: 8048383862.

The Turner Ashby Historical Society commemorates the life and times of Southern hero, Turner Ashby. Write to Patricia Walenista, 810 W. 30th Street, Richmond VA 23255, USA. Phone 8042323406.

The Immortal 600 Memorial Fund commemorates Confederate officers who have no marked graves. For details write to The Immortal 600 Memorial Fund, P.O. Box 652, Sparta, GA 31087.

Museums & Battlefields

Most American battlefields have visitor centres with museums and one of the most impressive, is at the Gettysburg Military Park. Many people are put off by the drive into Gettysburg because the town itself has become a tourist trap complete with a wax museum, but the uniforms equipment and artefacts in the visitor centre more than make up for this. The battlefield itself retains all the drama of the epic three day conflict, the largest ever fought on American soil. Walking across the scene of Pickett's charge is particularly memorable.

For brooding atmosphere though, the Antietam battlefield which has been relatively unspoiled by commercialism cannot be beaten, and it also has a fine visitors' centre, with many uniforms and artefacts on display. Twenty six miles southwest of Washington D.C. is the Manassas National Battlefield Park, encompassing both the first and Second battle. The visitor centre has good exhibits concentrating on the early period of the war, including the uniform worn by Corporal Brownell of the Fire Zouaves. The park also boasts a fine monument to Confederate general Stonewall Jackson. At Fort Sumter and Fort Moultrie in Charleston Harbour you can see where the war really began when the Confederates bombarded

Sumter. Both forts have been preserved very well and both have a selection of unusual artefacts.

Of the many Western battlefields, Shiloh Miltary Park in Tennessee comes highly recommended. The battlefield itself has almost the same atmosphere as Antietam and the well laid out visitors' centre boasts a wealth of exhibits.

A number of American museums such as the West Point museum at the academy in New York State boast an impressice collection of Civil War memorabilia. The U.S. cavalry Museum at Fort Riley, Kansas, has an impressive display of Civil war memorabilia and includes an extensive collection of saddles.

Urban areas also boast impressive museums, the Smithsonian in Washington D.C. boasts a fine collection of Civil War artefacts as does Fort Ward in Alexandra, Virginia, which was the fifth largest of the 68 forts manned to protect Washington during the Civil War. The G.A.R. Museum at 4278 Griscom Street, Philadelphia is another museum with some fine artefacts.

The Museum of the Confederacy at 1201 Clay Street Richmond VA 23219 is a must for both Yankee and Confederate military enthusiasts. The many artefacts include Jeb Stuart's plumed hat a Union Zouave's fez picked up at First Manassas and an impressive collection of flags.

To see where the war ended, a trip to Appomattox Court House, three miles east of the town of Appomattox in Virginia is a must. It was here that Lee surrendered to Grant and an impressive re-enactment of the Confederate surrender was made in the village in 1989. Today, Appomattox Court House has a brooding character all of its own.

For a flavour of Americam life in Britain, then a trip to the American Museum at Claverton Manor Bath is recommended. It's not specifically Civil War,but a large scale Civil War Battle is held behind the museum every year, in September.

Specialist tour operators run trips to American Civil War battlefields and the East Coast sites conviniently grouped together in Maryland, Pennsylvania and Virginia are at most a day's drive from each other. Holts' Tours Ltd, Brtitain's oldest specialist operator runs yearly trips to a variety of battlefields. Write to Holts' Battlefields & History, Golden Key Building, 15 Market Street, Sandwich, Kent CT13 9DA for details.

Civil War Book Suppliers

More books have been written about the American Civil War than possibly World War One and Two. Not only have many modern historians written about the American Civil War, but the era spawned numerous diaries and recollections of the conflict, as well as a steady stream of regimental histories in the years following the war. The following is a list of some leading American Civil War book suppliers.

Michael Haynes, 46 Farnaby Road, Bromley, Kent BR1 4BJ (Phone: 01814601672) sells a wide variety of Civil War books, both new and secondhand. Write or call if you want to be put on his mailing list.

Kennesaw Mountain Military Antiques, 1810 Old Highway 41 Kennesaw GA 30152 USA (fax 7704240434) offer a good range of new Civil War books and reprints including such gems as *Where Bugles Called* and *Rifles Gleamed*.

Broadfoot Publishing Company 1907 Buena Vista Circle, Wilmington NC 28405 USA (phone 8005375243, fax: 9106864379) has republished both the Army Official Records and the Supplement to the Official Records, indispensable books to any American Civil War enthusiast.

Olde Soldier Books Inc, 18779 B North Frederick, Gaithersburg MD, 20879, USA (Phone: 3019632929. Fax: 301963 9556) offers a wide selection of books, autographs, letters and documents.

First Corps Books, 42 Eastgrove Court, Columbia SC292122404, USA (Phone 8037812709) has a large selection of new and difficult to obtain out of print books.

Richard A. LaPosta 154 Robindale Drive, Kensington CT 06037 USA, (Phone 2038280921) specialises in regimental histories and has many first editions.

The Command Post Dept CN P.O. Box 141, Convent Station, NJ 079610141 USA (Phone: 800 722 7344) stocks many fine books.

Longstreet House, P.O. Box 730, Hightstown, NJ 08520 USA (Phone: 6094481501) specialises in books about New Jersey, Gettysburg and New York Civil War history.

The J.W. Carson Company (CWN) 130 Myrtle Street, Le Roy, New York, 144821332 promises to supply important Cuvil War books at affordable prices, including a reprint of the 1866 edition of Campaigns of the Army of the Potomac. 3,200

The Morningside Bookshop P.O. Box 1087 Dayton, Ohio, 45401 USA with a shop at 260 Oak Street, Dayton, Ohio 45410 (Phone: 18006489710) has one of the States largest selection of Civil War books and specialises in fine reprints.

Civil War Magazines & Newspapers

One of the finest Civil War magazines on the market is Military Images which features excellent articles and original pictures of Civil War soldiers. For subscription details write to Military Images Rt 1, Box 99A, Henryville, PA 18332, USA.

North South Trader, P.O. Drawer 631, Orange VA 22960 contains many fine articles on relic collecting and uniforms.

The Civil War News, Route 1, Box 36, Tunbridge VT 05077 USA,(Phone: 8028893500. Fax: 8028895627) is a monthly 'bible' on American and international Civil War events. The Civil War News also features an extremly useful small ads section and book reviews pages.

The Union Times, U.A.D.F. Publications 5330 County Road 561, Clermont, FL 34711 USA (Phone: 9043947206) covers the Civil War Seminole War and Mexican War in South Eastern America.

The Artilleryman, Rt. 1, Box 36, Tunbridge, VT 05077 USA (Phone: 8028893500) is a specialist magazine with articles on American Civil War artillery and artillery re-enactors.

America's Civil War, is a glossy magazine with plenty of intreest. Write to PO Box 383, Mount Morris Il 610547947 USA for subscription details.

In the same league is Civil War, the magazine of the Civil War Society, published by Outlook Inc, P.O. Box 770, Berryville, VA 22611, USA. Civil War Society membership details are also available from this address.

Artefacts

There are a number of good Civil War artefact suppliers, and even today some items can be picked up at reasonable prices.

The Union Drummer Boy, which has a correspondence address at 420 Flourtown Road, Lafayette Hill, PA 19444 USA and a shop at 5820 York Road, Lahaska PA 18931, offers a selection of excavated and non excavated relics. Their phone number is 6108256280.

R. Stephen Dorsey, Antique Militaria, at P.O. Box 263, Eugene OR 97440 USA (Phone: 5419373348) has a wide selection of guns and edged weapons.

The Powder Horn Gunshop Inc. P.O. Box 1001, 200 W. Washington Street, Middleburg, VA 22117, USA (Phone 5406876628) also has a wide range of items, including original belt plates.

One of the most famous centres for American Civil War artefacts is the Horse Soldier at 777 Baltimore Street, Gettysburg PA, USA (Phone: 7173340347) mailing address P.O. Box 184E, Cashtown PA 17310. A wide selection of goods are on offer and a catalogue is available at $15 for overseas customers.

Lawrence Christopher Civil War Relics, 4773 Tammy Dr. N.E., Dalton Ga 30721 USA (Phone: 8003368894 or 7062268894) has a selection of buttons, buckles, and bullets 3,600.

Civil War Videos & Art

Classic Images Productions International at PO Box 1863, Charlbury, Oxfordshire, OX7 3PD (Phone or fax: 01608676635) offers the entire range of Classic Images battle reenactment videos shot at anniversary events in America and featiuring thousands of reenactors in action. They also have *Echoes of the Blue and Gray Volumes One & Two*, actual footage of Civil War veterans shot after the war with some old soldiers actually describing their experiences. *Gettysburg 75th 1863-1938 The last Reunion of the Blue & Gray*, also has some rare colour footage of the combatants at Gettysburg meeting for the last time. Classic Images productions has become Britain's largest emporium of videos books and art and a catalogue is available.

Civil War art has become extremly collectable during the past decade and the dean of American artists is Don Troiani, whose limited edition prints are available from Historical Art Prints, P.O. Box 660, Drawer U, Southbury, CT 064880660, USA (Phone: 2032626680). Classic Images Productions International also hope to be stocking his work.

The Heritage Studio 2852 Jefferson Davis Highway, Suite 10912. Stafford VA 22554 USA (Phone: 5406591070 or 5408996675) stocks work by the artist Donna J. Neary who has a particularly vigorous style.

Limited edition prints by Don Stivers are available from Stivers Publishing, P.O. Box 25, Waterford VA 3,800 22190 USA.

Rick Reeves is another talented artist, whose work is available from Paramount Press Incorporated 1 West Main Street, Panama, NY 1467, USA (Phone: 7167824626)

Dale Gallon who specialises in action scenes, often opens his studio at 777 Baltimore Street, Gettysburg PA to the public. His prints are available from Dale Gallon Historical Art Inc. P.O. Box 43443, Gettysburg PA 17325 USA, (Phone: 717 334 0430).

Many businesses trade in Civil War art and one of the best known outlets for buying prints by Troiani and many other artists is Valor Art & Frame Ltd, 718 Caroline Street, Fredericksburg, VA 22401. USA. (Phone: 7033723376)

Stan Clark Military Books 915 Fairview Avenue (CWN) Gettysburg PA 17325 USA, (Phone: 7173371728, Fax: 717 3371728) also has a large selection of prints by Troiani and other well known artists.

Civil War Sculpture

Limited edition Civil War Sculptures have also become very collectable. The finest exponent of limited edition bronzes is Ron Tunison, who like Don Troiani is a member of the Society of American Historical Artists. Tunison began his artistic career just modelling one off clay figures, but there was so much demand for his work that he eventually turned to bronzes. Some of his most attractive and reasonably priced work is a series of busts of Civil War personalities, including George Armstrong Custer. For details write to Historical Sculptures P.O. Box 141, Cairo, NY 12413 USA. Phone: 5186223508.

Terry Jones is another fine sculptor particularly with his recent figure of Joshua L. Chamberlain. He can be contacted at 234 Hickory Lane, Newtown Square, PA 19073 USA. Phone 6103532210.

American Civil War Model Soldiers

Paul Clarke who runs Shenandoah Miniatures at 12 Holywood Grove, Carnegie, Victoria, 3163, Australia (Fax: 0116135341443) produces a fine range of 54mm American Civil War Figures. Particularly impressive is his range of Zouaves and Paul is planning some speciality figures in the range. To go with his figures, Paul also has an extensive spare parts list.

Tradition of London Ltd, 33 Curzon Street, Mayfair London, W1Y 7AE (Phone:01714937452. Fax:01713551224) has plenty of Civil War Figures in its range. Some, including a 14th Brooklyn figure were sculpted by Andrew C.Stadden. Tradition also has some sets of toy American Civil War figures, notably a set of 114th Pennsylvania Volunteer Infantry.

Chosen Men, 74 Rotherham Road, Holbrooks, Coventry, CV6 4FE (Phone or Fax: 01203666376) produce 120mm resin figure kits of a New

Black troops pose for camera in Virginia, November 1864. Peter Newark's Military Pictures.

Hampshire Volunteer, a Tiger Zouave and a Berdan's Sharpshooter.

Fort Duquesne Military Miniatures, 105 Tristan Drive, Pittsburgh, PA, 15209 USA, (Phone 4124861823) has an extensive range of figures and busts including a kit of an 83rd Pennsylvania Volunteer and a bust of a 155th Pennsylvania Volunteer, both sculpted by Gary Dombrowksi. Fort Duquesne Miniatures are available in Britain from Historex Agents, Wellington House, 157 Snargate Street, Dover, Kent CT17 9BZ.

Terry Worster Miniatures, 8529 Ablette Road, Santee, CA, 92071, USA (Phone: 6192581888) USA has a range of exquisite portrait busts incliuding U.S. Grant, George Meade and Thomas Meagher. He also carries a range of Civil War artillery models manufactured by Bayardi.

Michael Roberts Ltd, 2221 Hunters Road SW, Roanoke, Virginia 24015, USA (Phone: 5403427441 or 3432241) produces some fine figure kits, including a U.S. Army Brigadier General.

Index

Sutler's tent of the Federal Second Division, Ninth Corp. Peter Newark's Military Pictures / M. Brady.

Acknowledgments

The author would like to thank Richard Warren, Ron Field, David Scheinmann, Mike McAfee, Brian Pohanka, Martin Schoenfeld, and Richard O'Sullivan whose help was invaluable in writing this book.